Raising Rabbits

4th Edition

By Aaron Webster

© Rabbit Empire 2015 – All Rights Reserved

Forward:

Wind and clouds swirled through the skies with only the treetops blocking their incredible force. Way below the ferocious winds, there was a faint shadow of something running under the moonlit sky. The something carried a dim lantern and ran with weak but determined footsteps. A hurricane was coming and the footsteps belonged to me, a thirteen year old boy at the time who was desperately trying to protect his beloved rabbits...

My name is Aaron Webster and I have raised rabbits ever since I was ten years old. Over the years I have raised hundreds (probably thousands) of rabbits to sell to different markets. I enjoy wondering from time to time about how many living descendents of my rabbitry are currently populating the United States' rabbit farms. During the last couple years I have had the privilege of teaching quite a few people about raising, showing, breeding and selling rabbits. In January of 2011, I decided to create a huge United States based rabbit breeders directory (rabbitbreeders.us) with the purpose of helping others find and sell rabbits. Since then I have expanded the directory system... to include Canada and England. I enjoy spending time teaching others about raising rabbits, which is why I took the time to write this book. I have some pretty exciting ideas planned for this upcoming year, hopefully ideas that will help further the American and World rabbit industry! So stay tuned and enjoy the book! ☺

A photo taken of me at age 15, holding "Hope" the rabbit.

Introduction:

The first edition of Raising Rabbits 101 was initially published in June of 2011 with the purpose of providing the first time rabbit raiser with an easy to read but comprehensive guide to raising rabbits. Since then (in the latter two editions) this book has become a LOT more than just a getting started guide. Now Raising Rabbits 101 contains quite a bit of information and articles that even a rabbit guru would find useful.

This book is truly unique due to the fact that it is updated on a frequent basis, unlike most other rabbit books. The cool part about this book is the fact that upon purchase you will receive all updated digital eBook editions for FREE upon request! So basically once you purchase an eBook edition of this book you are entitled to a life time value of new rabbit information! I plan on publishing a new edition of this book on a yearly (or biyearly) basis… so I hope you can begin to see the true value of this book deal. **Note**: To purchase eBook and or softcover versions of this book visit: PremiumRabbits.com (the leading online rabbit supply store) or Amazon.com.

Good Luck and I Hope you Enjoy this Book,

Sincerely,

Author of Raising Rabbits 101

Aaron "The Rabbit Master" Webster

Rabbit Empire – Recent Book Publications

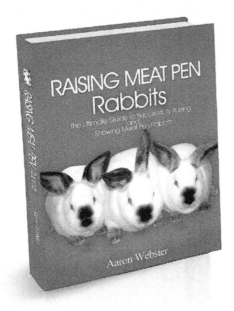 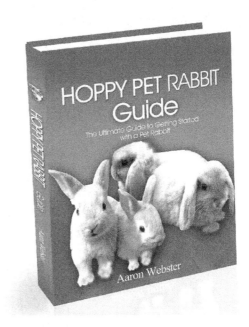

#1: Raising Meat Pen Rabbits

"The Ultimate Guide to Successfully Raising and Showing Meat Pen Rabbits"

Via Premium Rabbits: http://www.premiumrabbits.com/raising-meat-pen-rabbits/

Via Amazon: http://rabbitbreeders.us/AmazonMeatPenRabbits

#2: Hoppy Pet Rabbit Guide

"The Ultimate Guide to Getting Started with a Pet Rabbit"

Via Premium Rabbits: http://www.premiumrabbits.com/hoppy-pet-rabbit-guide/

Via Amazon: http://rabbitbreeders.us/AmazonPetRabbits101

Table of Contents

Forward: 2

Introduction: 3

Table of Contents 5

Part 1: Beginning Your Rabbit Adventure 9

    Rabbits around the World – An Intro to Rabbit Raising 10

    Reasons to Raise Rabbits 11

    Interesting Facts about Rabbits 13

    Choosing a Purpose 14

    Types of Rabbits 15

    Breeds of Rabbits Photo Gallery 21

    Breeds of Rabbits Chart 25

    Rare Rabbit Breeds 26

    Selecting a Breed 27

    Buying Rabbits 31

    Finding Rabbit Breeders 33

    Qualities of a Good Bunny Breeder 35

    Rabbit Supplies 36

    Purchasing Rabbit Supplies 38

    Rabbit Suppliers 39

    Getting Started - Overview 40

Part 2: Feeding, Breeding and Properly Housing Rabbits 42

    Feeding Your Rabbits 43

    My Feeding Method 44

    Rabbit Nutrition 47

    Rabbit Feed Brands 47

    Developing a Rabbit Feeding System 48

    Safe Rabbit Food List 49

    Unsafe Rabbit Food List 50

Feeding Tips, Tricks and Advice 51

Breeding Rabbits 101 52

Rabbit Breeding Schedule 53

How to Breed Rabbits 55

Breeding Help 57

Evaluating the Condition of Your Breeding Stock 59

Is My Doe Pregnant? 60

Breeding- Tips, Tricks and Advice 62

Kindling and Growing Bunnies 63

Preparing for Kindling 64

Breeding to Kindling and Beyond 65

Kindling and Birthing Problems 67

Additional Kindling and Bunny Growing Advice 69

Build Rabbit Housing 71

Building a Rabbit Barn 72

How to Construct a Rabbit Nest Box 73

Alternative Nest Box Design Plan 76

How to Build a Rabbit Cage 77

How to Build a Hay Feeder 79

Part 3: Rabbit Herd Management and Stock Evaluation 80

How to Sex a Rabbit 81

Parts of a Rabbit Chart 82

Evaluating Breeding Stock 83

Rabbit Identification 84

How to Tattoo a Rabbit 85

Pedigrees 101 87

Record Keeping 88

Blueprints for Growing and Expanding your Herd 89

Part 4: Rabbit Care Information and Advice 91

Rabbit Health 101 92

Signs that a Rabbit is Sick 93

Rabbit Diseases and Health Problems 94

    Health Problems: Symptoms, Causes, Treatments 95

Part 5: Marketing and Selling Your Rabbits 102

    Selling Rabbits Overview 103

    Rabbit Selling Outlets 104

    Deciding on a Fair Price 106

    Online Rabbit Advertising 107

    How to get your Rabbitry Featured Online 113

    Local Rabbitry Advertising 114

    Contact Management 115

    Developing a Good Reputation 116

    Additional Rabbit Revenue Streams 116

    How to Make Money Selling Fertilizer 117

    Make Money Growing and Selling Worms 118

Part 6: Interesting Resources + Additional Articles 119

    Raising Rabbits in the Sizzling Summer 120

    Raising Rabbits in the Winter 122

    Showing Rabbits 124

    Rabbit Color Genetics 127

    Managing Rabbits 131

    How to Handle a Rabbit 134

    How to Groom a Rabbit 137

    How to Transport a Rabbit 139

    Preventing Sore Rabbit Hocks 141

    Understanding Rabbit Pedigrees 144

    Rabbit Resources 146

    Final Words: 159

Part 7: Bonus Section and Glossary 161

    Bonus: Rabbitry Interviews 170

    Bonus: Rabbit Names List 171

    Rabbit Glossary 172

    Rabbit Terms and Definitions 173

Free Raising Rabbits Gift

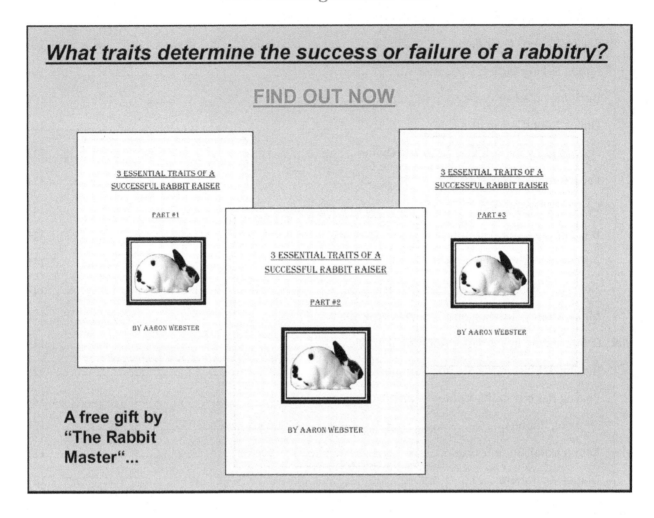

Free gift for you: Recently I put together a special report titled "The 3 Essential Traits of a Successful Rabbit Raiser". Today I would like to go ahead and give this report to you FREE OF CHARGE as a special gift from myself, "The Rabbit Master". In this special report I reveal to you the 3 traits that you need in order to become successful in the rabbit industry and provide you with information on how you can develop them if you don't already consider yourself to have these traits. To download your free copy of this special report you can visit: http://RabbitBreeders.us/essential-traits-download/ .

Part 1: Beginning Your Rabbit Adventure

Rabbits around the World – An Intro to Rabbit Raising

For thousands of years people from all around the world have been fascinated with the rabbit. The rabbit has found itself a place in many different cultures and has even been referenced in mythology written by the ancients. In Native American mythology for example, it was believed that the "Great Rabbit" was one of the important deities that created the world. The Aztecs also held the belief that there was a pantheon of four hundred rabbit gods which represented fertility, parties and drunkenness. In ancient Egypt the rabbit was used in a dog racing sport called "coursing". In the sport, a rabbit was used as a lure for the dogs to try and catch. This sport actually was continued in many different places, such as England until the nineteenth century when it was officially banned.

Just about everyone in western society has heard of the Easter Bunny. Over the years the celebration of Easter has been combined with a spring celebration which originated in Germany. The "death" of winter and the beginning of spring served as the basis for this celebration. Since the rabbit was seen as an animal which symbolized spring's fertility, it was adopted into the holiday celebration. This folklore celebration was brought to the Americas by settlers from Germany in the 1700s and has since continued to spread.

Due to the fact that rabbits can quite frankly "multiple like rabbits" under the right conditions, rabbits are commonly raised for their meat throughout the world. In many societies the "rabbit" has even become a primary source of consumer meat. Some research companies have estimated that approximately 34 million pounds of live rabbit is produced each year in the United States for the meat industry. Other countries such as Germany and Poland produce similar quantities of rabbit meat each year however they have significantly smaller national populations, giving them a bigger per capita rabbit consumption rate than the US. It is estimated that the world's largest rabbit producer is Italy, followed by Russia, China and France. China, however, has a smaller rabbit consumption rate per capita than the United States. Rabbit meat has proven to be one of the healthiest meats available for consumption boasting a high protein percentage and low amount of fat and cholesterol. Rabbits have been referred to by some as the "urban chicken" due to the fact that they require very little space to raise and can be produced almost anywhere. Many rabbit breeders point out however that rabbit meat is healthier than chicken and claim that the taste is much better. One of the biggest obstacles holding back the rabbit meat industry is the "Easter Bunny" image itself. A large number of people would simply refuse to try rabbit meat, thinking they were going to be eating some cute furry creature. Some breeders have pointed out that meat rabbits tend to be big and bulky not cute and furry… that however is a whole argument in itself.

The last two centuries have given birth to the rabbit showing industry, an industry that now includes tens of thousands of exhibitors worldwide. A main purpose of the showing industry has continued to be the development of better production animals for meat and fur. Today, many rabbit exhibitors are simply involved in the industry for a fun hobby. The industry now includes a very large number of youth rabbit fanciers who continue to raise and exhibit rabbits at local, state, and national rabbit shows. Organizations such as 4-H and FFA have helped to drastically spur the interest in raising rabbits and other animals amongst our society's youth.

During the last several decades the rabbit has been adopted into western society as a popular pet option. According to a statistic research firm, the third most popular pet in the country of England is currently the rabbit! (Beating out hamsters, fish, birds, snakes and mice!) I believe there are an even larger number of pet rabbits being kept in the United States; however the overall American pet population is also much larger. I personally know quite a few people who currently own or who have previously owned pet rabbits and that's just in my small town. It has been proven that pet rabbits can be house trained and live indoors just like the urban dog or cat, making them an enticing pet choice for many.

If my predictions hold accurate I believe that the rabbit industry will continue to grow in all aspects during this decade. More rabbits will be raised for meat, more rabbits will be taken to shows and lastly more rabbits will be raised for pets. I invite you to come take part in the excitement and begin your rabbit adventure!

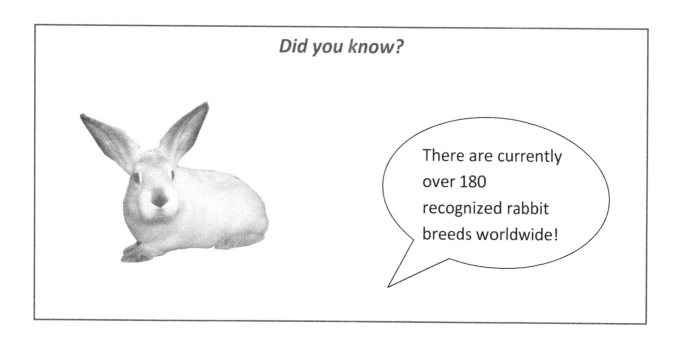

Reasons to Raise Rabbits

People from all around the world have chosen to raise domestic rabbits for a multitude of different reasons. Here is a list of **_11 reasons why you should consider raising rabbits_**...

Top Eleven Reasons to Consider Raising Rabbits...

1. **Rabbits are Low Maintenance**- One of the best things that I like about rabbits is the fact that they are relatively low maintenance animals.
2. **Rabbits are Quiet**- Yes I said it, rabbits are actually one of the quietest types of animals on the planet
3. **Economical**- Breeding rabbits can indeed be economical, even profitable if you put forth the time and dedication
4. **Rabbits can indeed "Multiply like Rabbits"**- Although struggling breeders will sometimes tell you different, rabbits can indeed multiply very quickly
5. **Rabbit Meat is Healthy**- Even if you never plan on eating rabbit meat yourself, if you breed rabbits you can rest assured that there is a market for rabbit meat in case you need to sell off stock or culls (you just need to have a good marketing plan in place- see part 5 of this book for information on selling rabbits)
6. **Rabbit Manure is Valuable**- Believe me when I say that rabbit manure works great as a fertilizer! Apply it to your garden and watch your plants bloom or bag it up and earn a little spending money off of it. ☺
7. **Rabbits Can Make Great Pets**- Rabbits can indeed make great pets- just make sure you choose the right breed or you might be disappointed!
8. **Self Fulfilling**- When you successfully breed rabbits you will most likely begin to feel self-fulfillment in your accomplishment (There is something about watching your rabbits grow that gives you a good feeling inside)
9. **Chance at Showing**- If you plan on showing rabbits, you will most likely have a great time and make some new friends!
10. **Great Learning Experience**- It would literally take an entire book to tell you about everything I have learned from raising rabbits!
11. **Raising Rabbits is Fun**- Most importantly raising rabbits can be a fun enjoyable experience as long as you do your research ahead of time (like read this book ☺)

Interesting Facts about Rabbits

In my opinion rabbits are a very amazing species. Here is a list of a few **interesting facts about rabbits**...

1. A Rabbit's teeth never stop growing!
2. The largest rabbit litter ever reported consisted of 24 bunnies!
3. Rabbits are classified as "lagomorphs"
4. The world's heaviest rabbit is Darius, weighing an unprecedented 50 pounds!
5. There are over 150 recognized rabbit coat colors and varieties
6. Rabbits only sweat on the pads of their feet
7. A group of bunnies from the same mother is called a "litter"
8. A rabbit will eat its own cecotropes (night droppings)- they are a valuable source of protein
9. Domestic rabbit kits are born with their eyes shut
10. Rabbits are nearsighted
11. A rabbit has five toenails on its front two paws and four toenails on its back two feet
12. In the wild rabbits live in groups called "warrens"
13. In ancient Egypt rabbits were used as sport for dog racing
14. There are around 180 different rabbit breeds worldwide
15. The longest rabbit ears ever recorded measured up to be 31.125 inches long!
16. Domestic rabbits are born without fur
17. Rabbits are not rodents
18. The backbone of a rabbit is very fragile and can break easily when handled improperly or dropped on its back
19. Rabbit males are called bucks and females are called does
20. Rabbits were an important home meat supply during World War II
21. The current world record for a rabbit long jump is 3 meters!
22. Hundreds of years ago rabbits were often released on deserted islands in hopes of giving shipwrecked sailors a reliable food source
23. Pet rabbits tend to live to be much older than wild rabbits
24. Rabbits have been commonly used as religious and mythical symbols throughout history
25. Rabbits and hares commonly found in the United States of America include the cottontail, jackrabbit, snowshoe rabbit and domestic rabbit

Choosing a Purpose

I believe the first step to beginning your rabbit adventure is "choosing a purpose". There are five main purposes for which people raise rabbits. I believe it is important to decide which category you would like to fall into before getting started. It is completely ok if you fall into more than one category... I know people who successfully raise rabbits for all five purposes.

- Show
- Meat
- Pets
- Fur
- Profit

Example: When I began my rabbit project the purpose of the project was to raise quality show rabbits. After about two years of raising rabbits, I began to sell quite a few rabbits to the meat market. Eventually my project evolved and producing meat rabbits became one of my main objectives.

As you shall soon see, your main purpose will influence all aspects of your rabbit expedition.

Photograph of a Californian Breeding Doe

Types of Rabbits

If you are looking to make your "rabbit experiment" a success the first thing you should consider after choosing a purpose, is selecting a rabbit breed which will fit your needs. In my opinion different types of rabbits might suit your purpose better than others...

Although there are many different ways to group rabbits, rabbit breeds are generally classified in three different ways; by body type, by fur type and lastly by body size. Each classification group will sometimes be referred to as a "type of rabbit".

One of the most popular ways to classify rabbit breeds is by the **rabbit's body type**. In fact this is the method that the American Rabbit Breeders Association uses to group breeds.

There are five different rabbit body types:

- Commercial – Best meat rabbit breeds, I also recommend selecting one of these breeds for show purposes
- Compact – I recommend these as pet breeds
- Cylindrical
- Full Arch
- Semi Arch – Giants

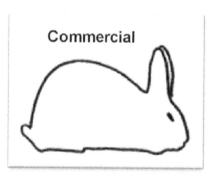

Commercial: Rabbits classified as having a **commercial rabbit body type** are rabbits with a gradual rise and fall up to the hips and down towards the tail. Rabbits in this category are generally very good meat rabbits due to their large loins and rapid growth rates. Some breeders have pointed out that these commercial breeds seem to look like a larger version of the "Compact Rabbits".

Commercial Breeds			
American Chinchilla	American Sable	Californian	Champagne d' Argent

Cinnamon	Crème d' Argent	French Angora	French Lop
Giant Angora	Harlequin	Hotot	New Zealand
Palomino	Rex	Satin	Satin Angora
Silver Fox	Silver Marten		

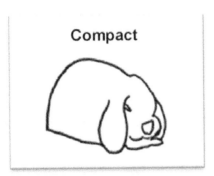

Compact: The small and medium rabbit breeds make up the **compact rabbit body type** category. These rabbits generally will look balanced when you pose them properly. When you run your hand over their bodies, your hand should gradually rise up across the rabbit to the hips and then curve itself smoothly down the rabbit to the tail.

Compact Breeds			
American Fuzzy Lop	Chinchilla	Dutch	Dwarf Hotot
English Angora	Florida White	Havana	Holland Lop
Jersey Wooly	Lilac	Mini Lop	Mini Rex
Mini Satin	Netherland Dwarf	Polish	Silver
Standard Chinchilla	Thrianta		

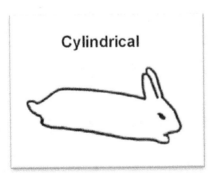

Cylindrical: According to ARBA, there is only one classified **cylindrical rabbit breed**. This group is made up of solely the Himalayan Rabbit. The Himalayan has the appearance of a Californian however is much smaller and of course cylindrical. When you judge this rabbit breed you should lay the animal out on the table in a "cylindrical" like fashion. See the picture above for a visual image.

Cylindrical Breeds			
Himalayan			

Full Arch: The **fully arched rabbit body type** is known for categorizing rabbits who sit in an "always alert" like fashion and who by coincidence seem to have a very energetic personality. These rabbits have straight erect ears and several have a spotted coat. Look at the image above.

Full Arch Breeds			
Belgian Hare	Britannia Petite	Checkered Giant	English Spot
Rhinelander	Tan		

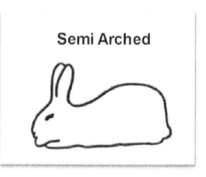

Semi Arch: The last remaining rabbit body type is the **semi arched rabbit**. Rabbits in this group tend to be large with low shoulders and a high hip. Some rabbit raisers will refer to this group as the "gentle giants". See the image above

Semi Arch Breeds			
American	Beveren	English Lop	Flemish Giant
Giant Chinchilla			

Another way rabbits are classified is by their fur type.

Types of Rabbit Fur
- Angora
- Normal
    - Flyback
    - Rollback
- Rex
- Satin

Angora Fur: There are six rabbit breeds which possess Angora, "Wool Fur". Wool fur is much like that of sheep fur however it has proven to be much denser.

Angora Fur Breeds			
American Fuzzy Lop	English Angora	French Angora	Giant Angora
Jersey Wooly	Satin Angora		

Normal Fur: Most rabbits are classified as having "normal fur". There are actually two different types of normal fur; Flyback and Rollback.

- **Flyback Fur:** When a rabbit has flyback fur its coat will "fly back" into place after being petted backwards.

Flyback Fur Breeds			
American Belgian Hare	Britannia Petite	Californian	Champagne D' Argent
Checkered Giant	Cinnamon	Crème D' Argent	Dutch
English Lop	English Spot	Florida White	French Lop
Giant Chinchilla	Harlequin	Havana	Himalayan
New Zealand	Palomino	Polish	Rhinelander
Silver	Silver Marten	Tan	

- **Rollback Fur:** Rollback fur is longer than flyback fur and will "roll back" into place after running your hand against it.

Rollback Fur Breeds			
American	American Sable	Beveren	Dwarf Hotot
Flemish Giant	Holland Lop	Hotot	Lilac
Mini Lop	Netherland Dwarf	Satin	Silver Fox
Standard Chinchilla			

Rex Fur: Rex Fur is a fairly rare type of rabbit fur that is only found in two rabbit breeds; the Rex and the Mini Rex. Rex Fur is of a soft and velvety texture.

Rex Fur Breeds			
Mini Rex	Rex		

Satin Fur: There are only two breeds which possess "Satin Fur". These breeds include the Satin and Mini Satin. Satin fur is much softer than normal fur.

Satin Fur Breeds			
Mini Satin	Satin		

Rabbits are commonly **classified by size** just like body type and fur. For the purposes of this book I am going to categorize the different breeds of rabbits into **four average weight groups**;

- Small – Under six pounds (2.7 kg)
- Medium – Between six pounds (2.7kg) and 9 pounds (4.1kg)
- Large – Between 9 pounds (4.1kg) and 11 pounds (5kg)
- Giant – Over 11 pounds (5kg+)

Small Breeds: In my opinion these small breeds make the best pets or show animals for small children. These breeds generally weigh less than six pounds and are easy to handle.

Small Breeds			
American Fuzzy Lop	Britannia Petite	Dutch	Dwarf Hotot
Florida White	Havana	Himalayan	Holland Lop
Jersey Wooly	Mini Lop	Mini Rex	Mini Satin
Netherland Dwarf	Polish	Silver	Tan

Medium Breeds: These medium sized rabbit breeds make a great choice for somebody desiring a rabbit not too small but at the same time not too large. Medium breeds can be used as multipurpose animals, breeders raise these breeds for all different purposes; meat, show, and pets. These animals generally weigh between six and nine pounds.

Medium Breeds			
American Sable	Belgian Hare	English Angora	English Spot
French Angora	Harlequin	Lilac	Rex
Rhinelander	Satin Angora	Silver Marten	Standard Chinchilla

Large Breeds: I personally recommend that you decide to purchase a large breed animal if you are planning on raising rabbits for either meat or show. These animals tend to be easy to care for, healthy and productive. When full grown these large breeds tend to weigh between nine and eleven pounds.

Large Breeds			
American	American Chinchilla	Beveren	Blanc de Hotot
Californian*	Champagne D' Argent	Cinnamon	Crème D' Argent
English Lop	French Lop	Giant Angora	New Zealand*
Palomino	Satin	Silver Fox	

*indicates my favorite breeds from the category

Giant Breeds: These breeds of rabbits are referred to by some breeders as the "luxury breeds". Many times these huge animals are raised specifically for show reasons. I wouldn't recommend that you raise these giant breeds for meat due to the fact that they have a lower percent dress out rate than most of the Large Breeds. Some breeders however have experimented with cross breeding a giant breed such as the Flemish Giant with a large breed to increase meat production. The size of these "Gentle Giants" continues to amaze me.

Giant Breeds			
Checkered Giant	Flemish Giant*	Giant Chinchilla	

*indicates my favorite breeds from the category

Breeds of Rabbits Photo Gallery

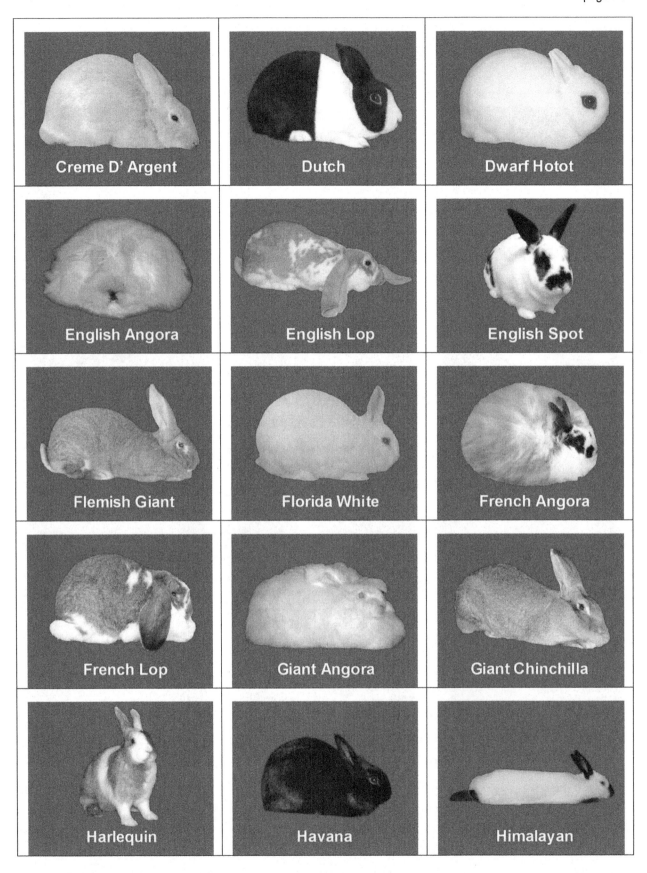

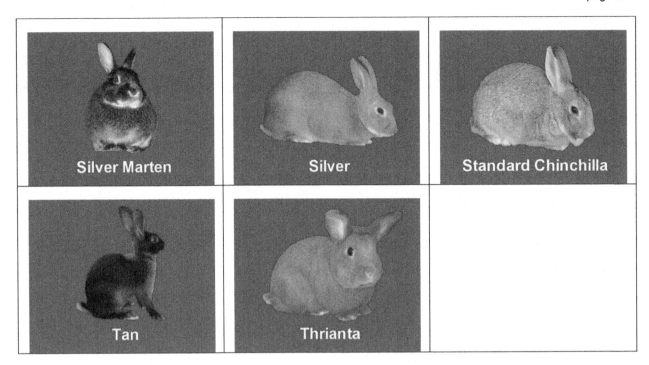

Breeds of Rabbits Chart

Here a list of the 47 different ARBA recognized rabbit breeds. Information from the types of rabbits section is summed up in this chart.

\multicolumn{5}{c}{Breeds Summary Chart}				
Breed	**Weight**	**Size**	**Body Type**	**Fur**
American	10-11 lbs	Large	Semi Arch	Flyback
American Chinchilla	9-11 lbs	Large	Commercial	Rollback
American Fuzzy Lop	3.5-3.75 lbs	Small	Compact	Angora-Wool
American Sable	8-9 lbs	Medium	Commercial	Rollback
Belgian Hare	6-9.5 lbs	Medium	Full Arch	Flyback
Beveren	8-11 lbs	Large	Semi Arch	Rollback
Blanc de Hotot	8-11 lbs	Large	Commercial	Rollback
Britannia Petite	2.5 lbs	Small	Full Arch	Flyback
Californian	8-10 lbs	Large	Commercial	Flyback
Champagne D' Argent	9-11 lbs	Large	Commercial	Flyback
Checkered Giant	11.5 + lbs	Giant	Full Arch	Flyback
Cinnamon	8-11 lbs	Large	Commercial	Flyback
Crème D' Argent	8-11 lbs	Large	Commercial	Flyback
Dutch	3-5 lbs	Small	Compact	Flyback
Dwarf Hotot	2.5-3 lbs	Small	Compact	Rollback
English Angora	6-9 lbs	Medium	Compact	Angora-Wool
English Lop	9-10 lbs	Large	Semi Arch	Flyback
English Spot	6-8 lbs	Medium	Full Arch	Flyback
Flemish Giant	13 + lbs	Giant	Semi Arch	Rollback
Florida White	4-6 lbs	Small	Compact	Flyback
French Angora	6-9 lbs	Medium	Commercial	Angora-Wool
French Lop	10.5-11 lbs	Large	Commercial	Flyback
Giant Angora	9-11 lbs	Large	Commercial	Angora-Wool
Giant Chinchilla	12-15 lbs	Giant	Semi Arch	Flyback
Harlequin	6.5-9 lbs	Medium	Commercial	Flyback
Havana	4.5-6 lbs	Small	Compact	Flyback
Himalayan	3-5 lbs	Small	Cylindrical	Flyback
Holland Lop	3-4 lbs	Small	Compact	Rollback
Jersey Wooly	3-3.5 lbs	Small	Compact	Angora-Wool
Lilac	5.5-7.5 lbs	Medium	Compact	Rollback
Mini Lop	4.5-6 lbs	Small	Compact	Rollback
Mini Rex	3-4.5 lbs	Small	Compact	Rex
Mini Satin	3-6 lbs	Small	Compact	Satin
Netherland Dwarf	2-2.5 lbs	Small	Compact	Rollback
New Zealand	9-11 lbs	Large	Commercial	Flyback
Palomino	9-10 lbs	Large	Commercial	Flyback
Polish	2.5-3.5 lbs	Small	Compact	Flyback
Rex	7-9 lbs	Medium	Commercial	Rex
Rhinelander	6-9 lbs	Medium	Full Arch	Flyback
Satin	9-11 lbs	Large	Commercial	Satin

Satin Angora	6-9 lbs	Medium	Commercial	Angora-Wool
Silver	4-6 lbs	Small	Compact	Flyback
Silver Fox	9-11 lbs	Large	Commercial	Rollback
Silver Marten	6-9 lbs	Medium	Commercial	Flyback
Standard Chinchilla	5-7 lbs	Medium	Compact	Rollback
Tan	4-6 lbs	Small	Full Arch	Flyback
Thrianta	7-9 lbs	Medium	Compact	Rollback

Rare Rabbit Breeds

Some of these 47 rabbit breeds are labeled as being "rare" by the American Livestock Breeds Conservancy. Here is a list of the rarest 11 breeds: (labeled in 3 levels of rarity). Rarity is measured by a list of factors including; Yearly ARBA breed registrations, National Breed Club Reports and information provided by individual breeders.

Critical:
- ❖ American
- ❖ American Chinchilla
- ❖ Silver Fox

Threatened:
- ❖ Belgian Hare
- ❖ Blanc de Hotot
- ❖ Silver

Watch:
- ❖ Beveren
- ❖ Crème d'Argent
- ❖ Giant Chinchilla
- ❖ Lilac
- ❖ Rhinelander

To learn more about the American Livestock Breeds Conservancy or their standards, visit their website at: *albc-usa.org.* If you would like to support the organization or help one of the individual breeds grow in numbers, consider raising one of these rare breeds.

Selecting a Breed

Selecting a rabbit breed is definitely one of the most important decisions that you will make for your rabbitry. Luckily for you, there are over 47 different breeds of rabbits to choose from. This is when you will want to recall the "purpose" that you decided on at the beginning of this book. Any rabbit breeder will tell you that some breeds are definitely more ideal for different purposes...

Things to Consider When Selecting a Rabbit Breed
- Purpose of your Rabbitry
- Rabbit Size
- Rabbit Body Type
- Type of Fur
- Color/Markings
- Growth Rate/Litter Production
- Your Climate (is it too hot or too cold?)

Meat Rabbit Breeds

If you plan on raising rabbits for meat I strongly recommend that you choose a large "commercial" rabbit breed which will produce fast growing offspring with a good meat to bone ratio. I personally recommend raising Californians or New Zealands as meat rabbits. They grow fast; have large litters and overall make excellent "meat rabbits".

Here is a list of "for meat" rabbit breeds that many different breeders recommend
- American Chinchilla
- Beveren
- Blanc D'Hotot
- Californian (My favorite breed)
- Champagne D'Argents
- Crème D'Argents
- Flemish Giants (Giant animals but tend to have lower meat to bone dress out ratios)
- Florida White
- French Lops
- New Zealand (Highly Recommended)
- Palomino
- Satin
- Silver Fox

Some breeders recommend raising a crossbred animal such as a Californian-New Zealand hybrid for meat purposes.

One of the most popular hybrid rabbit meat breeds is the Altex (Although not recognized by ARBA). The Altex was developed from a cross of the Flemish Giant, Champagne D' Argent and Californian. At adult size these cross bred rabbits weigh between 10 and 20 pounds. Studies performed at the Texas A&M University have shown that Altex fryers tend to reach market age earlier than other meat breeds. Many rabbit breeders however don't recommend that your primary herd animal be the "Altex" for several reasons. The Altex doe will generally give birth to smaller litters than other meat rabbits. To solve this issue, many breeders recommend breeding an Altex buck to a Californian/New Zealand doe or an Altex doe to a New Zealand buck.

Show Rabbit Breeds

If you plan on primarily raising rabbits for show, you will have an excellent variety of breeds to choose from! All 47 ARBA recognized breeds are eligible to be shown at any major rabbit show. However be warned; most local shows will not accept every breed. If you plan on raising up one of the "rare" breeds such as the Blanc de Hotot; you might have to drive a distance in order to find available shows.

A good practice when choosing a show breed is to ask other breeders in your area for their opinion on selecting a breed. In Southeast, Texas for instance most breeders raise Californians or New Zealands. They are multi-purpose animals which can be shown at two different types of rabbit shows; Meat Pen Rabbit Shows and Rabbit Fancier Shows. Even if you don't plan on eating rabbit yourself, raising either one of these breeds will help guarantee that you have an outlet to sell unwanted rabbits.

Here is a list of "for show" rabbit breeds that many different breeders recommend

- American
- Californian
- Dutch
- Flemish Giant
- Lilac
- Lop (any breed)
- Mini Rex
- New Zealand
- Palomino
- Polish
- Satin
- Tan

These are simply a few recommendations that breeders have given me... if you fall in love with a different breed (not on the list), feel free to experiment! ☺

Fur Rabbit Breeds

Most breeders agree on what the best fur rabbit breeds are. If you are choosing to raise rabbits particularly for fur, I highly recommend that you select a breed labeled as having either having wool or angora fur. The most popular "for fur" breed is the Angora Rabbit.

Here is a list of "for show" rabbit breeds that many different breeders recommend
- American Fuzzy Lop
- English Angora
- French Angora
- Giant Angora
- Jersey Wooly
- Satin Angora

Pet Rabbit Breeds

In many countries rabbits are quickly becoming one of the most common pets. When choosing a "for pet" rabbit, I suggest that you select one of the small or medium breeds. These animals will generally be tamer than the larger breeds such as the Californian and will be easier for young children to handle. Remember, the best production animals don't usually make the best pets.

Here is a list of "for pet" rabbit breeds that many different pet bunny owners recommend
- Belgian Hare
- Cinnamon
- Dutch
- Dwarf Hotot
- English Spot
- Flemish Giant (Size is great for impressing a friend ☺)
- Harlequin
- Himalayan
- Lionhead (Not yet ARBA recognized)
- Lops (My favorites are the Holland and Mini Lops)
- Mini Rex
- Mini Satin
- Netherland Dwarf (So tiny and cute ☺)
- Rex
- Tan
- Thrianta

Also if you are planning on raising rabbits for pets, it is important to consider whether or not you want to breed rabbits. If you are new to rabbit raising and plan on breeding for pets, you might want to start off with a medium breed (they tend to have less birth complications than smaller breeds). Some small breeds such as the Tan and Mini Satin are still great choices for the first time breeder. Just make sure the breed that you choose weighs over 4 pounds at adulthood.

Buying Rabbits

The **rabbit buying process** has a reputation for overwhelming the first time rabbit raiser. Sometimes a rabbit enthusiast will fail to purchase a desired rabbit breed due to the fact that they are unable to locate any available stock. Many times people don't even know where to begin looking for rabbits. Sometimes people take a guess at where they should buy and later regret their decision...

Popular Places to Buy Rabbits From
- ❖ Pet Shops
- ❖ Flea Markets
- ❖ Rabbit Rescue Centers
- ❖ Backyard Rabbitry Breeders
- ❖ Dedicated Rabbit Fanciers & Hobbyists

Pet Shops

One of the most popular places to buy pet rabbits seems to be from the local pet store... You probably remember walking through the pet store as a little child looking at all the cute little animals. Maybe you still do! I remember the "pet store" used to be my favorite stores in the entire mall to visit. Maybe you asked a family member multiple times... "Can I keep him.. He is sooo cute; yes of course I will take good care of him".

Just like puppies, kittens and mice, rabbits are frequently sold in pet stores to unprepared owners. Although they are a popular pet store animal I would not recommend buying them from a pet store. I have heard of multiple people who have had bad experiences with purchasing bunnies from pet stores. Unfortunately one of the reasons behind this is the fact... that pet store owners don't tend to know very much about caring for rabbits. Sure they might know everything there is to know about dogs and cats but generally not rabbits.

Rabbits will frequently die after being brought home from pet stores due to lack of care. Also another factor behind the general poor health of pet store bunnies is the fact that they are usually taken off their mothers too early. Pet stores tend to want to buy "small" rabbits, many times "too small" of rabbits.

Conclusion: STAY AWAY FROM PET STORES

Flea Markets

Another popular place to find bunnies is Flea Markets. I personally have never purchased rabbits from a Flea Market and quite frankly don't intend to for the following reasons:

Reason 1: Normally Flea Market Rabbits are of mixed rabbit breeds... if you are thinking about ever showing your rabbits this is a bad idea. Also, most of the time rabbits found there will not be the ideal meat rabbit stock.

Reason 2: You do not know the history of where these bunnies came from... what were their previous living conditions? Are they truly healthy bunnies? Why did the breeder sell them? - For all you know these rabbits could be the culls (undesirable ones) of a litter.

Reason 3: You will not be able to get pedigrees on your bunnies... the fact of the matter is Flea Market Rabbits generally have zero chance of coming with pedigrees... an essential part of record keeping.

Reason 4: You will not be able to contact the breeder with questions... this is an important advantage of buying from a rabbit fancier.

Conclusion: Yes, Flea Markets might be a great place to find cheap rabbits however I strongly recommend that you look elsewhere for rabbits.

Rabbit Rescue Centers

Rabbit Rescue Centers are generally good places for adopting a rabbit. Often you can save a life by deciding to adopt a bunny.

One thing I want to point out about shelters and rescue centers is the fact most of the bunnies would not be suitable for showing or breeding for meat. In fact many rabbits taken to shelters are automatically spayed or neutered.

I personally would not recommend getting a rabbit from a shelter. There simply are better places to find quality bunnies.

Conclusion: If you want to try and help an abandoned bunny find a lost home, shelters may work great for you. If you are looking for breeding rabbits or show stock – this is definitely not a good option.

Backyard Rabbitry Breeders

One of the better places to buy rabbits is from Backyard Rabbitry Breeders. These breeders tend to be small time rabbit raisers and usually keep between three and twenty rabbits at a time.

They generally know at least the minimal information needed to care for their bunnies properly. So on average rabbits bought from them will be in better health.

Conclusion: Backyard Rabbit Breeders are one of the better places to find rabbits. My best recommendation however is to buy from serious rabbit hobbyists and fanciers.

Dedicated Rabbit Fanciers & Hobbyists

My number one recommendation regarding buying rabbits… is to buy from Serious Rabbit Hobbyists and Fanciers. These are the dedicated people who normally have larger rabbitries and generally know a lot more about their breeds.

These are the type of people who will frequently go out of their way to make sure you have everything you need to care for your bunnies.

Conclusion: Buy from serious rabbit hobbyists and fanciers… although you will most likely have to pay more for your bunnies this way, I can almost guarantee that "the investment" will be worth it in the long run.

Finding Rabbit Breeders

So now you may be wondering; "Where can I locate these dedicated rabbit fanciers & hobbyists?" Years ago I was asking myself this exact question. After days of desperately calling around asking breeders, I was able to locate a breeder about 120 miles away from my house that had a trio of rabbits for sale. Believe it or not, I was very lucky that year to find breeding rabbits available during November in southeast Texas.

In December of 2010 I came up with a great idea to help people find local rabbit breeders. I started a huge rabbit breeder's directory network with the purpose of helping connect rabbit breeders and buyers. Although at the time there were already many established online breeders directories, none of them seemed to be big enough to really make a significant impact. What is the use of a Wisconsin based rabbit breeder's directory to the average rabbit enthusiast living in Texas? I also noticed that a large number of the directories on the web, were way outdated. So I decided that I was going to accept the challenge and provide this online directory service to worldwide rabbit breeders free of charge.

To date the main directory site RabbitBreeders.us has received upwards of 2,500 rabbitry submissions from the United States alone!

Initially I started two separate websites RabbitBreeders.ca and RabbitBreeders.org.uk to cover Canada and the United Kingdom respectively; however I have since combined these sites into the single RabbitBreeders.us to reduce maintenance costs and make upkeep easier.

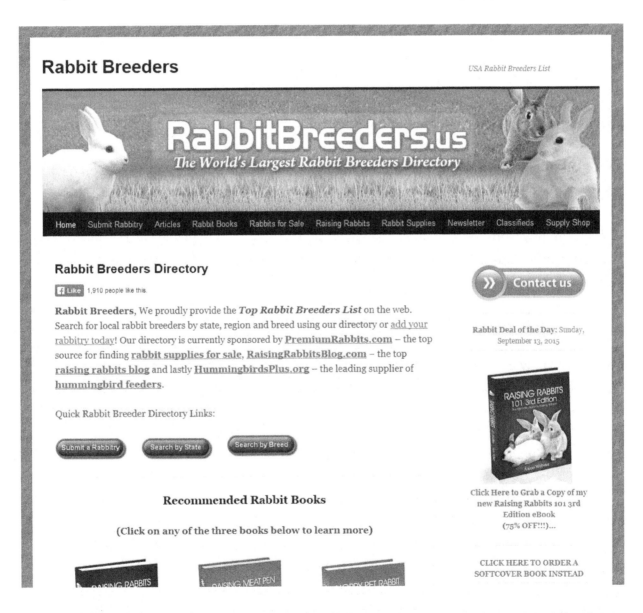

The site contains two main directory indexes; State/Province Breeders Index and Breed Index. Using these two directories you can either find rabbit breeders by location or specific breed.

I strongly recommend that you use RabbitBreeders.us to find local rabbit breeders. The directory network is growing extremely fast, in fact I already have had hundreds of rabbitry submissions in the last couple months alone. Currently most of these submissions have been from our USA Rabbit Breeders Directory which now contains over 2,500 rabbitry listings! Although they are relatively small at the moment, we do anticipate growth in our newer Canadian and England based rabbit breeder directories within the upcoming months and years.

I have been astonished with the wonderful feedback that I have received from many of the rabbit breeders with rabbitries listed in our directories! I guess my time building and maintaining these directories was well worth it. ☺

However what has been accomplished so far is just the beginning of what I have planned for the next few years! To keep track of what I am planning, you can visit RabbitBreeders.us and subscribe to our free email based newsletter.

Quick Links / Resources

Free Rabbit Breeders Newsletter: http://rabbitbreeders.us/rabbit-breeders-newsletter
Locate Rabbit Breeders: http://rabbitbreeders.us/
Submit your Rabbitry: http://rabbitbreeders.us/free-rabbitry-submission
Update Rabbitry Listing: http://rabbitbreeders.us/update-rabbitry-submission

---

Qualities of a Good Bunny Breeder

What are traits that "Good Bunny Breeders" exhibit? I have noticed that the best bunny breeders tend to exhibit the following traits:

Trait #1: Know their material- these breeders tend to have a firm grasp on raising rabbits and understand their breeds well
Trait #2: Willing to provide Assistance- reputable breeders will usually be willing to help answer some of the questions you have about raising and caring for rabbits
Trait #3: Give you evaluations of the rabbits you are buying- the best breeders will give you an honest evaluation of the rabbits that they are selling you
Trait #4: Have a good reputation- obviously if a friend recommends you to a rabbit breeder saying how awesome they are, there is a very good chance that the statement is true
Trait #5: Nice people- generally the "best bunny breeders" tend to be nice folk in general

Rabbit Supplies

If you are new to rabbit raising you are probably wondering; **What supplies do I need to buy for my rabbits?** Here is a **list of supplies that successful rabbit breeders recommend that you purchase**:

For a Production Animal

-Rabbit Cage or Hutch
-Quality Rabbit Pellets
-Rabbit Feeder
-Rabbit Water Bottle or Automatic Watering System
-Bag of Rabbit Hay
-Some type of transportation device- rabbit carrier
-Book on Raising Rabbits (this book will do ☺)
-Rabbit Tattoo Clamp
-Digital Scale
-Rabbit Nest Box

For a Show Rabbit

-Rabbit Cage or Hutch
-Rabbit Carrier
-Rabbit Food – preferably pellet based
-Rabbit Feeder
-Some Hay for your Rabbit
-Rabbit Water Bottle or Bowl
-Rabbit Grooming Supplies
-A Good Rabbit Care Book (this book will do ☺)
-Rabbit Tattoo Clamp
-Digital Scale
-Rabbit Nest Box

For a Pet Rabbit

-Rabbit Cage or Hutch
-Pet Rabbit Carrier
-Bunny Rabbit Food – organic or pellet based

-Rabbit Bowl or Feeder
-Rabbit Hay
-Rabbit Toys
-Bedding and Litter
-A Great Pet Rabbit Care Book
-Digital Scale

Some of the supplies listed above are essential to the well being of every one of your rabbits. Every grown rabbit that you buy will need to have its own rabbit cage or hutch compartment to reside in. Also once your rabbits reach three months of age (or before they reach breeding age- breeding age may vary based upon breed) you will need to separate males and females. For every cage that you buy you will need to make sure that you purchase either a rabbit feeder or bowl for food and a water bottle or bowl to hold your rabbit's water supply. You also will need to make sure that you have enough food and hay for your rabbits to consume.

You don't need to purchase a carrier for each of your rabbits unless you plan on transporting all of them at once. If you plan on showing your rabbits, they can share show grooming supplies. Well obviously unless you plan on teaching your rabbits to read, you will not need a rabbit care book for each rabbit! ☺

Rabbit Cage vs Rabbit Hutch – What is the Difference?

When buying rabbit housing supplies people always seem to ask;
What is the difference between a cage and a hutch?

Answer: Basically rabbit cages and hutches are the same thing. Most people intermix the two terms. Generally speaking however hutches tend to be larger structures made out of wood. Cages on the other hand usually are made out of all-wire or wire and plastic enclosures. If you do a search on Google Images you most likely will see similar results for both searches.

Purchasing Rabbit Supplies

There are many different places that you can purchase rabbit supplies. Some of these places offer reasonable prices, others do NOT! If you don't know better you could end up paying double the price that someone else like me pays for the exact same item. So before I recommend rabbit suppliers and stores... here is a chart including information on what you can expect to pay for each item.

Please Note: If you buy items in quantity you will generally be entitled to lower prices than the ones listed below.

Basic Rabbit Supply Cost Chart	
Item	Average Price
Rabbit Cage	$75-100
Rabbit Hutch	$120-250
Rabbit Carrier	$20-60
Bag of Rabbit Feed	$6-15
Rabbit Feeder	$5-10
Rabbit Water Bowl	$5
Rabbit Water Bottle	$5-10
Bag of Rabbit Hay	$10
Rabbit Tattoo Clamp/Kit	$30-55
Nest Box	$15-25
A Good Rabbit Care Book	$20
Bag of Rabbit Litter (Pet Rabbits)	$8
Rabbit Toy (Pet Rabbits)	$5

How Much Will It All Cost?

Well assuming the costs listed above... the initial supply costs for one rabbit would be approximately $200. For three rabbits the cost would be approximately $280. Generally you will save money on supplies when you buy quantity. You also have the option to make some of your own supplies for a lower price. (see part 2 of this book)

Generally the highest cost item that you will need is the cage or hutch. Price varies heavily on these two items due to the fact that they come in all different sizes, shapes and styles. Where a basic rabbit cage might cost around $75 at the normal supply store, a two compartment cage might cost only a little bit more. Hutches generally cost more because they are made out of wood. Buying multiple compartment housing structures will definitely help save you money in the long run.

Rabbit Suppliers

To find rabbit supplies for sale at affordable prices check out our recommended rabbit suppliers and dealers below...

Recommended Rabbit Suppliers and Dealers:

#1 Recommendation: PremiumRabbits.com

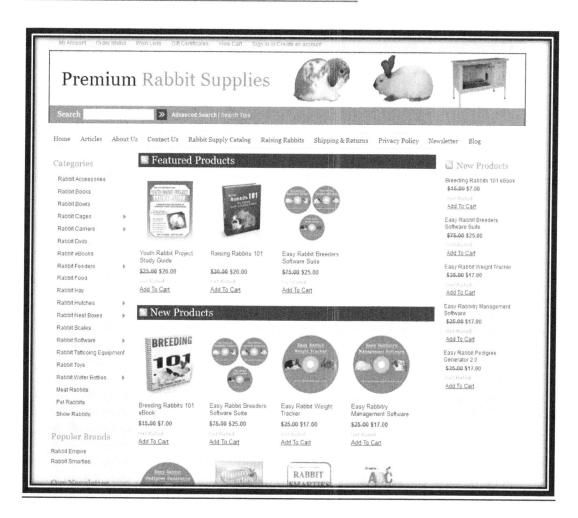

Amazon Rabbit Supply Store – rabbit hutches, cages, feeders, books, bottles, etc...
-Visit Store: **RabbitBreeders.us/Amazon**

Note: If you are willing to invest time and effort you can build some of your rabbit supplies yourself to save money. (See Part 2 of this book for building instructions)

Getting Started - Overview

Hopefully by now you are ready to begin your rabbit adventure. In Part 1 of this book we covered the basics to getting your "hands wet" into the rabbit world.

You now should be able to effectively choose a rabbit breed to fit your purpose, locate local rabbit breeders and purchase the right supplies for your rabbit(s).

I provided you with a rabbit breed reference chart and photo gallery which you are free to print out or use at any time. These two resources should have aided you in your decision regarding rabbit breed selection. If you are still unsure of what breed you would like to purchase, read over the material again or try to get advice from family members. It is ok, you can take your time. The best thing you can do for yourself and your future rabbit(s) is to do the appropriate planning.

Photo Credit: Giancarlo Cuciz "The Rabbit King"

I suggest that if you have already decided on a breed, that you take advantage of the links I have provided you with to begin searching for local rabbit breeders. Sometimes it can take awhile to find the right rabbits. In the process, it would be a good idea to begin purchasing supplies for your rabbits. (See Page 39 for purchasing links)

Photo Credit: Tara Tedjarati and Family

In Part 2 of this book we will be covering; Feeding, Breeding and Rabbit Housing in depth. By the end of the section you will have information at your fingertips which should allow you to construct rabbit cages and nest boxes with the purpose of saving money. You will also learn tips and tricks which will help you better manage your rabbit expedition.

Part 2: Feeding, Breeding and Properly Housing Rabbits

Feeding Your Rabbits

Most people have false assumptions about what domestic rabbits really eat. Many people are hooked on the idea that you should feed your rabbits lots of carrots and lettuce. WRONG!!! Don't get me wrong it is ok for rabbits to occasionally eat carrots and lettuce however it should not makeup their main diet. Studies have shown that feeding rabbits lots of vegetables can get them over fat and contribute to other health conditions.

If you are into raising rabbits for production or show I highly recommend that you feed your rabbits a quality pellet based feed. A quality pellet based feed will help your rabbits grow quickly and stay in good health. Rabbit pellets generally contain all the vitamins that your rabbits will need, so you will not have to worry about vitamin supplements.

Pellet vs Natural Feed

When I tell people that I recommend feeding rabbits grain instead of natural rabbit food, the statement often leads to controversy. Particularly people who fit into the raising "urban pet rabbit" category often moan and complain, saying that natural (non-pellet based) food will help your bunny rabbits live longer. I have yet to find any real evidence behind this claim, in fact the healthiest rabbit food I currently know of (RabbitBreeders.us/SherwoodForest) is pellet based.

If you have a large herd of rabbits it is much more time and cost efficient to feed pellets than it would be to gather food stuff for each of your rabbits on a daily basis. As long as the feed contains appropriate levels of protein, fiber, fat and vitamins you can rest assured that your rabbits are being fed a healthy diet. If you are still obsessed with the idea of feeding your rabbits a combination of veggies, hay and other more natural foods each day instead of pellets, be warned that you will have to consistently make sure that your rabbits are getting all of the important ingredients that they need from the mixture.

When Natural (Non Pellet Based) Food is the Best Solution

In some situations feeding non pellet based foods to your rabbits could prove to be the best solution. If you have a productive garden and are trying to become as self-sufficient as possible, feeding more natural foods might prove to be worth the effort. You may be able to reduce your feed bill and be better off if tragedy was ever to strike. Your rabbits wouldn't be dependent upon the big corporate farms which produce crops necessary to grain production. During both World War I and World War II rabbits were commonly raised for backyard meat production in order to feed starving families. One thing I want to point out is the fact that during any major crisis, food prices are notorious for soaring. Sometimes crops are damaged and as a result livestock feed would also soar in price. (I hope you are able to see my point here)

Conclusion

So after considering both points of views... here is my conclusion: Initially start your rabbits off on a pellet based feed. If you wish after a few weeks, you can begin to introduce and supplement more natural food for pellets. Make sure you do this process gradually, if you switch feeds too quick your rabbits could get stressed and go off their feed altogether. For show rabbits I still recommend a strictly pellet diet, with hay as a dietary supplement.

My Feeding Method

I primarily raise Californian Rabbits for show and commercial purposes. Each day I feed my rabbits a food ration of approximately 5 to 6oz of pellet feed each. They also have access to hay on a consistent basis. Occasionally I will feed them grass or certain types of leaves for a treat. Personally, I don't feed my rabbits any veggies.

The Measuring Cup and Distribution

To equally distribute out my feed on a daily basis, I use a classic Dixie cup as the scoop. Each rabbit will get 1 to 1.5 scoops per day, depending on whether or not they ate all their food up from the previous day. Occasionally I will go around my rabbit buildings with a bag of hay and place a small handful in each cage for my rabbits to munch on. Some of my older cages contain built in hay holders, however this is not a necessity. Several online stores such as Amazon sell hay racks that can clip onto your rabbits' cages to help keep the hay contained.

5 oz Dixie Cup- Feed Scoop   Bag of Petros Rabbit Grain   Rabbit Food Bucket

When I occasionally feed my rabbits grass treats, I will use a small pair of clippers to cut the grass instead of pulling it up. I only will give each rabbit as much grass as they will eat within a few minutes. Wilted grass is not good for rabbit consumption.

Water the Most Important Ingredient

The most important ingredient in any rabbit feeding system is old classic H_2O! Rabbits must have access to a consistent supply of water at all times in order to stay in good health. In the summer if a rabbit goes without water for more than a few hours it can become detrimentally ill and even die.

The best solution for supplying your rabbits with a constant water supply is to use an automatic watering system! The majority of backyard rabbit raisers however simply use bowls and water bottles to hold their rabbit's daily water supply. I could go on and on about the pros and cons to different watering methods however I don't want to bore you. So here is a short paragraph which sums up the differences...

In the old days before the development of specialized rabbit supply products, most people used bowls to hold their rabbits' food and water. Now the majority of rabbit raisers have began using water bottles that hang onto the rabbits' cages. There are two main types of rabbit water bottles; Flip-Top and Screw-Bottom (see below for a visual image). Flip Top bottles will save you time due to the fact that you don't have to take them off the cage to refill. Flip Top bottles however tend to be more expensive than the typical screw bottom rabbit waterer. Using water bottles instead of bowls will generally save you maintenance time and keep your rabbits' water supply cleaner. Lastly there are automated rabbit watering systems. These systems will definitely save you time however they will also take an investment of both time and money to setup.

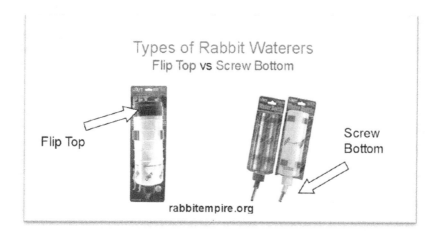

Water Transportation

If you have a good number of rabbits, you will need to come up with a solution for transporting water to your rabbit enclosure. I have it setup so that a water hose runs from my outside water faucet to my rabbit buildings. I then have the hose attached to another faucet which I use to manually distribute water to my rabbits. I also use the same faucet pipe to run my automatic watering system.

If you are going to manually distribute water to each of your rabbit cages, I suggest that you use 2 gallon milk or water jugs. They are simple, hardy and best of all free to use water hauling devices. I remember when I first started raising rabbits I used plant watering containers to fill rabbit bowls! (That was a joke- use milk jugs instead ☺)

Rabbit Feeders

So now that we have discussed rabbit watering devices, it is time to talk about rabbit feeders. I recommend that you purchase "J Feeders" for each of your rabbit cages. J Feeders are simply metal feeders that hang on the outside of your rabbit cages which allow you to distribute food from the outside of the rabbit cages. Special rabbit feeders are MUCH better than bowls for several reasons; they save you time, they keep your rabbit's food cleaner and rabbits can't flip them over like they can bowls.

To distribute rabbit grain each day I use a simple carrying bucket and a 5oz Dixie cup. I keep my open rabbit grain bags in metal trash cans to keep rodents and moisture away from the grain. I store the rest of my rabbit grain bags in a stack in my garage.

Note: J Feeders can be purchased via http://www.premiumrabbits.com/rabbit-feeders/ .

Rabbit Nutrition

Rabbits need to have a balanced diet. It is important to pay attention to the contents of your rabbit feed. Some things to pay particular attention to include; protein, fiber and fat percentages.

Protein plays a major role in helping your rabbits grow and stay in good health. Many breeders recommend feeding your breeding does a higher protein feed than the rest of your herd to help with milk production. I personally feed all my rabbits an 18% protein feed. I could feed all my bucks a 15% protein feed however from my experience it is easier to simply keep all your animals on the same feed. The store that I buy my grain from usually prices their 18 and 15% feed at about the same price, so it isn't like I am spending more money by feeding all by animals the 18% feed.

Next you want to make sure that you pay attention to the fiber content in the feed. Fiber is important in helping your rabbits digest their food and keep their gut moving. I personally feed my rabbits an 18% fiber grain. If you wish you can supplement a lower fiber feed with some grass hay. Hay is also a good source of fiber for rabbits.

Lastly, it is a good idea to pay attention to the amount of fat that the feed contains. The grain that I feed my rabbits contains about 2.5% fat. If your rabbit feed contains too much fat there is a good chance that your rabbits will get overweight. If your breeding does get too fat their chance of producing large litters of kits is greatly reduced. Some fat is important though; fat is one of the key ingredients which help your rabbits grow a nice fur coat.

Rabbit Feed Brands

Here is a list of some of the most popular rabbit feed brands:

- ❖ Petrus (this is the brand that I feed most my rabbits) : RabbitBreeders.us/Petrus
- ❖ Sherwood Forest Natural Rabbit Food (recommended - highest quality feed I currently know of – feed to my indoor pet rabbits): RabbitBreeders.us/SherwoodForest
- ❖ Purina
- ❖ Manna Pro

Quick Tip: If you have a hard time locating any of these brands in your area, try asking other local breeders what they feed their rabbits.

Developing a Rabbit Feeding System

Each individual rabbit raiser is responsible for developing a rabbit feed system which works for both them and their rabbits. Although I can give you advice which can help make your feeding program a success, it is ultimately up to you to make the decisions. Hopefully these guidelines will help you out...

Feeding: Time of Day

I recommend that you feed your rabbits in the evening if possible. Rabbits are naturally more active in the nighttime and will eat most of their food up during this time of the day. Especially if you live in a humid climate because rabbit grain that sits in feeders for too long will grow moist; this may cause your rabbits to snub their nose at it.

Quick Tip: If you are unable to feed during the evening I suggest that you feed during the early morning hours. (A rabbit's second most active time of day)

Multiple Meals a Day?

In my opinion feeding rabbits multiple times a day is unnecessary. Once a day feedings; will generally be adequate enough.

Quick Tip: Before a meat pen rabbit show, exhibitors will often feed their rabbits multiple times a day in order to help their rabbits gain additional weight. Sometimes just the act of somebody going out to the rabbit hutch and "stirring things up" helps encourage eating.

Free Feed or Ration?

Many rabbit fanciers have started debates about whether or not rabbits should be free fed or rationed. My answer to the question is; it depends. I don't recommend that you free feed your entire herd; not only will many of your rabbits get overweight but your feed bill will also "get heavier". I suggest that instead you free feed only your mothers with growing kits and the bunnies themselves.

Note: Above are just a few simple guidelines that I suggest you follow. You are free to do whatever you want, this is your "rabbit experiment" not mine.

Safe Rabbit Food List

Below I have included a list of plants, flowers, twigs, vegetables, leaves, herbs and grains that have been labeled by rabbit experts as being "safe for rabbit consumption". Please note however, I have not had the chance to test out all the foods on my rabbits. If your rabbit happens to get sick after eating one of these items neither me or Rabbit Empire shall be held responsible.

Herbs, Grains, Vegetables

- Alfalfa
- Apple
- Banana
- Barley
- Basil
- Blackberry
- Broccoli
- Buckwheat
- Carrot
- Celery
- Clover
- Corn Marigold
- Cow Parsnip
- Cucumber
- Dandelion
- Melon
- Oats
- Parsley
- Parsnip
- Peppermint
- Pumpkin
- Raspberry
- Sage
- Tomatoes
- Watermelon
- Wheat

Leaves

- Apple
- Beech
- Birch
- Blackberry
- Cherry
- Hazel
- Mulberry
- Pear
- Raspberry
- Strawberry

Flowers

- Carnation
- Daisy
- Geranium
- Hollyhock
- Marigold
- Rose
- Sunflower

Twigs

- Apple
- Birch
- Blackberry
- Fir
- Hazel
- Hawthorn
- Maple
- Pear
- Raspberry
- Willow

If you are ever in doubt about one of the substances ask another rabbit raiser in your area. I seriously doubt any of these items listed above would ever harm your rabbits, however like I said above I have not had the chance to test out all of the substances.

Quick Tip: A good way to test out new foods on your rabbits is to use moderation and only give them a tid-bit to begin with.

Unsafe Rabbit Food List

Here is a list of foods that are labeled as being "unsafe" for rabbit consumption...

Herbs, Grains, Vegetables, Other
- Bindweed
- Bluebell
- Buttercup
- Chocolate
- Cowslip
- Evergreens
- Hemlock
- Kingcup
- Milkweed
- Scarlet Pimpernel
- Peach/Plum leaves
- Potato Sprouts

Twigs
- Apricot
- Azalea
- Beech
- Cherry
- Ivy
- Mistletoe
- Oak
- Peach
- Plus
- Rosewood
- Thorn Apple

Flowers
- Acacia
- Columbine
- Daffodil
- Dahlia
- Iris
- Larkspur
- Poppy
- Tulip

Of course there are many other plants and foods that rabbits shouldn't consume however this is a list of some of the most popular foods that make rabbits sick.

Quick Tip: I recommend only feeding your rabbits foods that are listed on the safe list or foods that you have seen other breeders feed their rabbits.

Feeding Tips, Tricks and Advice

Here is a list of feeding tips and tricks that I have assembled:

1. Feed your rabbits some type of hay on a frequent basis.
2. The most effective rabbit food is a nice pellet based feed.
3. If you are raising rabbits for show, I suggest that you ask around your area to see what other successful rabbit breeders are feeding their rabbits.
4. I have found it effective to slightly increase a doe's feed ration at about two weeks before she is bred.
5. Don't over-feed your does or you might not get any bunnies!
6. Evaluate the contents of a rabbit feed bag before making a purchase.
7. Growing bunnies will generally stay healthiest when they are free fed.
8. Keep your bucks well fed, but don't get them too fat or they won't breed as well.
9. When a doe has a litter of bunnies to nurse; try giving her an unlimited feed ration.
10. It is a good idea to keep your rabbits on the same feed without changing brands too often.
11. If a rabbit isn't eating its pellets try feeding him or her some green grass.
12. Sometimes if a rabbit doesn't eat much of its food, it could be a sign that something is wrong with their water supply.
13. Don't feed your rabbits candy or sweets. If you want to feed them treats check out your rabbit supplier's catalog for "rabbit safe treats".
14. It is important to gradually decrease a doe's feed when weaning a litter of bunnies.
15. In the summer rabbits will generally consume less food.
16. If you show your rabbits I suggest that you limit their daily intake of vegetables. For instance, give carrots as treats not as a main meal course.
17. The most noticeable sign that a rabbit could be ill is when it stops eating.
18. If you consistently change out your rabbits' diet, be sure to keep a notebook of the changes that you have made. This way if something goes wrong you will hopefully be able to diagnose the problem.
19. When buying rabbits from a breeder, be sure to ask them what brand of food they feed with. Some breeders may be able to sell you enough feed to last until you can visit the feed store.
20. "A well fed and active rabbit is generally a healthy rabbit."

Breeding Rabbits 101

Rabbit breeding is one of the most significant factors that will help determine the long term success of your rabbitry. As we all know rabbits can be excellent breeders, however many rabbit raisers struggle with getting their rabbits to breed for several different reasons. So this chapter is basically about "The art of getting rabbits to breed like rabbits".

Reasons to Breed Rabbits

It is always best to start out an in-depth topic like this with the basics. So to start with, here is a short list of reasons why people breed rabbits in the first place.

- The process of raising and caring for baby bunnies can be a fun and interesting learning experience
- Rabbit Breeding can be a profitable enterprise
- Many rabbit shows judge rabbits at market age, so exhibitors need to have approximately 10 week old bunnies to be eligible to show
- Rabbit meat is proven to be one of the healthiest meats available for consumption
- Bunny rabbits make excellent photography subjects
- Around Easter each year there is a high demand for pet rabbits

Things to Consider Before Breeding

Throughout my years of raising and breeding rabbits I have learned an important lesson; it is critically important to take into consideration a few factors before making the big decision to breed. Here is a list of several things you should consider before breeding...

- Successfully raising up bunny rabbits will require a dedication of time and labor
- Rabbit rescue centers are filled with unwanted rabbits
- Many first time rabbit raisers find it difficult to get rid of excess rabbits
- Bunnies will grow up quickly and require more space (so be prepared)
- You will need to purchase or make a nest box for each doe that you breed
- No matter what you do, bunnies will occasionally die (this is the reason that rabbits are made to have such large litters)
- In case of a crisis, you will have to problem solve to save your bunnies (hopefully this book will provide you with enough information to make the right decisions)

Rabbit Breeding Schedule

If you are anything like me, you are probably wondering when you should breed your rabbits. I believe one of the most important parts of rabbit raising is herd management, which includes developing a breeding schedule. Here are some guidelines and a breeding calendar to assist you in your decision...

Do Rabbits Have a Breeding Cycle?

If you have raised any other livestock animal you will probably realize that animals tend to have a breeding cycle. Their fertility and willingness to breed is often determined by this cycle. As a goat raiser it is important for me to pay close attention to these cycles in order to determine when is the best time to bring a doe to the Billy goat. The good news is from my experience rabbits don't tend to have a breeding cycle. Some rabbit raisers have claimed that rabbits tend to have a 3 to 4 day cycle each month where their chance of getting pregnant is minimal. I believe that as long as you have a healthy doe and an eager buck cycles don't really matter much. I want to point out the fact that some female rabbits living in the wild will get pregnant up to eight times a year! So this fact makes me question the authenticity of breeding cycles.

When Should I Breed?

If your purpose behind raising rabbits is to produce home grown meat for your family or simply to raise rabbits for pets, then for the most part you will have the luxury of deciding when you want to breed your rabbits. Now for the majority of us rabbit raisers, we will have to breed at certain times of the year whether we want to or not. If you plan on showing rabbits at meat pen shows then you will be required to breed your rabbits almost on an exact day in order to produce kits the right age for the show. Secondly if your goal is to raise rabbits for profit, it is important to take into account market considerations when deciding when to breed. Some markets will only accept bunnies at certain times of the year while others will demand bunnies year round.

The ideal seasons to breed your rabbits include; spring, fall and winter. If you live in a cooler climate such as the northern United States, summer can also be a great option however winter may not be. Rabbits thrive best in mild climates which is one of the reasons why California has become such a popular place to raise rabbits. Unfortunately the majority of us will have to make do with the climates that we live in and do our best to work around the forces of Mother Nature. Since I live in Southeast Texas my biggest obstacle is the scorching summer heat. I however get a reprieve of not having to worry much about brutal winters. Rabbits on the other hand tend to prefer cold climates over hot climates. In order to understand this statement, picture yourself being stuck in a fur coat in the summer time. Rabbit fur serves to be a great insulator of heat. (Great for the fur industry, but bad for the average southern climate rabbit)

How Often Should I Breed?

In order to keep your rabbits in good breeding health you need to breed your rabbits at least three times a year. If you fail to breed your rabbits enough your does can build up internal fat in their uterus, which will reduce their chance of getting pregnant or simply reduce their average litter size in general. Although many commercial rabbitries will breed their does six times a year, for the general rabbit raiser it is best to breed your does between 3 and 4 times a year. I personally breed all my does three times a year.

How Long Does a Rabbit's Gestation Cycle Take?

From personal experience I have noticed that in general a rabbit's gestation cycle lasts approximately 30 days from breeding to kindling. In general a good rule of thumb is that a rabbit pregnancy cycle will last between 28 and 32 days. Of course if you raise rabbits long enough you are sure to find an exception. Just a few weeks ago I had a doe that had bunnies 36 days after being bred! This type of variation is extremely rare with rabbits, maybe 34 days but 36? Most of the litter died due to the fact that I already removed the nest box from the doe's cage (assuming that the doe was not going to have bunnies).

Rabbit Breeding Calendar

In part 7 of this book you will find a cool rabbit breeding calendar which I created to help you figure out when your bunnies should be born in accordance to the day that you bred your does. The calendar also shows you which day you should place a nest box into your doe's cage. You are free to print the calendar out and keep it with your rabbit records.

How to Breed Rabbits

As many rabbit raisers will tell you, there are several steps involved in the process of successfully breeding rabbits. Hopefully this article will help give you a better understanding of the process.

Step 1: Develop a Breeding Plan – in order for your rabbitry to be successful you must develop a successful plan for breeding your rabbits. This plan should include when you plan on breeding, the does and bucks that you intend to breed with and the purpose behind the breeding.

Step 2: Animal Evaluation- it is a good idea to look over the animals that you plan on breeding to make sure that they are in good health and condition. Good healthy does will generally produce nice healthy kits. A doe that lacks condition will many times have smaller litters with smaller kits in general. It has also been noticed by many rabbit breeders that the buck's condition also plays a role in producing quality kits.

Step 3: Getting Started- In order to begin the breeding process, locate the doe that you wish to breed and bring her to the buck's cage.

Step 4: The Breeding- There are several different rabbit breeding methods that successful rabbit raisers use. One method involves simply placing the doe in the buck's cage and the other involves manually restraining her. The majority of successful rabbit breeders that I know choose to use the restraining method to help guarantee pregnancy.

Restraining Method: This method is also commonly referred to as the "Forced Mating Method". If you choose this method simply place the doe inside of the buck's cage and gently put one hand over her head and the other underneath her so that she can't run around the cage. If everything goes right the buck should mount her and then fall off signaling that the mating was successful. If both animals are agreeable the mating should only take about 30 seconds or less. Most of the time if the mating is going to occur it will happen in the first two minutes. If you are using an inexperienced buck you can try to gently place him on top of the doe to help him get the hint.

Watch and Wait Method: I refer to this method as the Watch and Wait Method due to the fact that this is your main job during the breeding. If you select this method you will simply place the doe in the buck's cage and then close the cage door. The buck will then hopefully make an effort to chase the doe around his cage and mount her. Once he has mounted and bred her you can remove the doe from his cage.

Step 5: Contain the Doe- Some studies have shown that if a doe urinates after the mating she can unintentionally foil the pregnancy. There is a good chance that if you place the doe right back in her cage after the mating she will urinate immediately due to the fact that she is overwhelmed. So many breeders suggest placing the doe in an enclosed box or cage other than her own for about twenty minutes after a successful mating. I have observed that the doe won't normally urinate unless she is in her own cage. I personally keep my does inside of wooden nest boxes after they are bred. Before using the nest boxes to enclose does I initially put them inside an old gerbil cage will a glass bottom.

Step 6: Record the Mating- make sure that you write down either the ear tattoos or names of both the doe and buck that you bred together. When it is time to breed my does I create a list of all the does that I plan to breed and the bucks that I plan to breed each doe to on a large piece of cardstock paper. Once I breed the does I place a small x on top of the date that the mating occurred. This recording system will help me remember when I need to place a nest box in the cage for the bred doe. Remember as I said before one of the keys to a successful rabbitry is a successful management system.

Step 7: Rebreed the Doe- In order to help guarantee that a doe is pregnant you should breed her to a buck at least three times. If you only have a few does and need to have bunnies born for a show I recommend that you breed each doe a minimal of six times each. It is best to breed your does in the morning and then once again in the evening. Some breeders also encourage breeding a doe more than once within the same hour to help take advantage of egg stimulation. If you are new to rabbit raising I know this breeding process may sound a bit extensive however it necessary if you need to guarantee that kits are born within a certain time frame. One breeder that I knew recommended that a rabbit raiser breed each of their does 12 times each! In my opinion this is unnecessary and also too time consuming; however it is recommended that you breed each of your does at least three times apiece.

Breeding Help

If I just had a dollar for every email or question that I have received from people who were having trouble getting their rabbits to breed I would indeed be a rich man. So I thought it would be a good idea to give you some pointers on how to get troublesome rabbits to breed. Hopefully after reading this article you will be a better equipped rabbit breeder.

My Doe Won't Breed

Most of the time breeding issues will arise from your does not wanting to breed rather than your buck; generally the biggest obstacle is getting your younger does bred.

Breeding Tips/Tricks:

- The single best way to get your does to breed is to use the "Restraining Method" that I talked about in the last article.
- Make sure you keep your does in great condition (for information on evaluating breeding condition see page 59) and up to ideal breeding weight. For large rabbit breeds such as the Californian and New Zealand the ideal breeding weight for a doe is about 8.5 pounds +.
- Try to keep your does calm during the breeding process. I have found that if you set them on the table and stroke them gently for a few minutes before bringing them to the buck's cage they will tend to be more cooperative.
- Ideally try to keep your does in a fairly cool environment before attempting to breed them. Intense heat unnecessarily stresses out your animals.
- Always bring the doe to the buck's cage and not vice versa. As I have mentioned before does are naturally very territorial and generally will fight the buck if he is brought to their cage.
- Some breeders recommend moving a troublesome doe to the buck's cage the night before attempting to breed and moving the buck to a different cage. The theory is that the doe will acquire some of the buck's scent and will be more agreeable to breed the next day.

My Buck Won't Breed

It can be very discouraging when you find out that your buck won't breed. Most the time this issue seems to arise at the time when you need him to breed the most. Don't ask me why this seems to happen, it just does as most experienced rabbit raisers will tell you.

Breeding Tips/Tricks:

- My best advice regarding breeding rabbits is to make sure that you have at least two breeding age bucks at all times. This way if one decides not to breed, you will have a backup. Most breeding issues seem to arise when people only have one buck.
- Make sure your buck is old enough to breed! The fact of the matter is that some bucks take longer to mature than others. For larger rabbit breeds; I recommend getting a buck that is at least 9 months old. If you get lucky you might find that some bucks will be ready to breed at as young as 3 months of age.
- Check beforehand to see whether or not your buck's reproductive sack has descended to a visible state. If you flip your breeding buck over and can't tell right off that he is a buck you have a problem.
- Try to keep an experienced buck that has already produced offspring in your herd at all times.
- Sometimes keeping a doe living inside the cage beside the buck will keep him in a breeding mood.
- If you are breeding a timid buck for the first time try to breed him to one of your more agreeable does. This will help him build "breeding confidence".
- Some bucks do not like humans standing nearby watching them breed. If you find a buck like this try standing to the side where you are not standing in the buck's view, but are still able to evaluate the mating.
- Keep your bucks in a cool environment if possible. Bucks can go sterile for a couple months in the summer if they are not kept cool enough.
- If you need to breed your bucks in the summer, be sure to keep them breeding on a consistent basis. The theory behind this is the fact that this will keep your bucks producing fresh sperm and help them avoid becoming sterile.

Evaluating the Condition of Your Breeding Stock

From personal experience I have noticed that one of the key factors that determine the success of a breeding is the condition of your breeding stock. The condition of your breeding stock will greatly affect the quality and quantity of offspring produced from a specific breeding. Here are some pointers which will help you determine the condition of your breeding stock...

- Some Signs of poor condition include; skinny animals, mites in ears, loss of weight, fur mites, sore hocks, pink eye, extensive loss of hair, runny nose, diarrhea, etc
- Signs of a rabbit in good condition include; good breeding weight, good fur condition, clear eyes, clean ears, happy looking rabbit

I have noticed that rabbits in poor condition will generally act unwilling to breed. If a rabbit in poor condition has bunnies the litter will usually be smaller in size and won't grow as fast as normal.

Below are a few pictures which should help you evaluate the condition of your breeding stock:

Good Condition:

 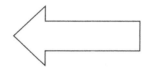

Notice the fullness of body, healthy looking face, ears and eyes.

Poor Condition:

Notice that this doe is too skinny and overall lacks condition. If you look closely you will notice that this doe has an abscess on her face.

Quick Tip: If you have rabbits in poor condition try to diagnose the cause of their lack of condition. If a rabbit is sick take the appropriate measures to treat the illness before breeding with that animal.

Is My Doe Pregnant?

So now that you know how to breed your rabbits you may be wondering whether or not you can tell if your doe is pregnant. If you have some extra time on your hands it is quite possible to at least make an educated guess. Although less obvious than larger animals, rabbits do indeed show several signs of pregnancy...

Rabbit Pregnancy Signs

- The doe begins to gain weight
- The doe begins to eat less about a week before her bunnies are due
- Several days before her bunnies are due the doe begins putting hay into her nest box
- The doe pulls fur from her chest and places it in her nest box
- You notice the doe panting intently

Can I Tell for Sure?

If you notice your doe placing hay in her nest box I would say there is about a 75% chance that she will indeed deliver bunnies. If she pulls fur and starts making a nest in the nest box the chance increases to 90% or higher. If you wish to know whether your rabbit is for sure pregnant I suggest that you weigh her at the time of the breeding. Within a couple weeks weigh her again, if she has gained a good amount of weight there is a high indication that she is indeed pregnant. A good practice to help guarantee the accuracy of this test is to weigh other rabbits in your herd at the same time that you weigh the doe. This will allow you to evaluate if the weight gain was due to a factor such as weather or whether it is indeed an indicator of pregnancy.

Another Method

Another method rabbit raisers use to determine whether or not a doe is pregnant is the "breed test method". This method is based upon the theory that a doe tell whether or not she is pregnant. A rabbit breeder will place the doe that was bred the previous week back into the buck's cage. If the doe gets all upset and starts grunting or trying to attack the buck, then it is a reasonable assumption that the doe is already pregnant. Again this method is based upon theory not fact...

False Pregnancies

Just like humans rabbits can have "false pregnancies". Many times human mothers that really want to have another child will begin to get all excited when they see familiar changes in their body. Sometimes these women will go to a doctor only to find out it was simply a "false pregnancy". Although I highly doubt that a rabbit's false pregnancy has anything to do with emotion, they can indeed experience them. I have had several "falsely pregnant" does go as far as making a beautiful nest, only they never delivered a litter.

Professional Method

Most likely your rabbit isn't going to be taken to the doctor to have a special pregnancy test done like a human mother, so you may be wondering whether there is any way that you can know for sure. The keyword to answering your question is "palpation".

Palpation is the process of feeling a rabbit's belly to determine whether it is pregnant.

Steps to Successfully Palpating a Doe

1. Around day 12 of a rabbit's pregnancy you should be able to successfully palpate a doe. Until then you will just have to hold tight because it is difficult to notice any other signs this soon into the pregnancy.
2. Move your doe to a flat surface, a rabbit judging-evaluation table works nice.
3. Pick her up with one hand and use the other to gently feel around the sides of her belly.
4. If you feel any "grape-like" balls along the sides of her belly they are most likely little kits!

Palpation does take a lot of practice. I advise you to get with a rabbit raiser in your area to go over the process with you on one of their pregnant does. This will help you to get the hang of what you are feeling for.

Quick Tip: Try feeling the belly of a doe that you know isn't pregnant side by side the doe that you are trying to palpate. Hopefully this will help you notice a difference if the doe that you are palpating is indeed pregnant.

Breeding- Tips, Tricks and Advice

Here is a summary list of rabbit breeding tips and tricks that I have assembled:

1. You should breed your does at least three times a year in order to help maintain their breeding health (if you fail to do so, your does may build up too much internal fat and not be able to have bunnies at all).
2. When breeding your rabbits always bring the doe to the buck's cage and not vice versa (a doe can be very territorial).
3. Breed your rabbits multiple times over a several day period (especially if you have only a few does).
4. Do NOT leave the doe in the buck's cage for longer than 5 to 10 minutes.
5. Restraining the doe in the buck's cage is a technique many experienced rabbit breeders use (known as the Restraining Method).
6. If you breed your rabbits during the warmer months of the year, make sure that you keep your main bucks active and breeding in order to keep fresh sperm in their systems (Bucks can go sterile for periods of time when they are kept in constant heat above 85 degrees Fahrenheit).
7. If you want to know whether or not your does are pregnant try palpating them about two weeks after they are bred.
8. On average a rabbit's gestation cycle will last 30 days from breeding to kindling.
9. It is best practice when breeding your does to bring them to the buck at least twice on the breed date.
10. Some bucks are better breeders than others so choose your bucks wisely. One of the factors that should determine whether or not you keep a buck is by how well he breeds.
11. Generally "experienced bucks" will breed better than the first time breeders.
12. The prime breeding age for most bucks is between 1 and 3 years of age.
13. Rabbits can indeed have "false pregnancies" (a false pregnancy occurs when a doe falsely thinks that she is pregnant and possibly even goes as far as pulling fur or making a nest).
14. Make sure that your breeding rabbits have unlimited access to fresh water.
15. Most bucks don't reach breeding age until six months of age.
16. Does in superb condition will be more likely to produce nice healthy offspring than does that lack condition.
17. A doe generally will be old enough to breed at six months of age. (breeding age may vary based upon the breed and size of the animal)
18. Lastly, be sure to keep good breeding records!

Kindling and Growing Bunnies

So once you have bred your does it is time to start thinking about birthing and kindling bunnies. Hopefully if you follow the guidelines presented in this section, you will have a successful experience raising up your own bunny rabbits.

The Excitement

One of the most exciting moments of your rabbit career is getting your first litter of bunnies. It is neat to watch a determined doe make a beautiful nest out of hay and fur. I believe that it is amazing that a mother rabbit can make such a talented creation inside of a nest box.

Watching and Waiting

The baby bunnies are actually born without fur. You will get to see cute pink little kits crawling around in the nest box during nursing time. Hopefully each day the kits will grow just a little bigger and begin to put on a layer of fur. After awhile you will notice that your kits have begun to open their eyes. Before you know it you will have cute and furry little bunnies crawling out of the nest box. Once the bunnies start hopping out of the nest box they will begin to eat and drink with their mother. At about four weeks old the kits will begin eating a good deal of rabbit food each day. The kits will begin to grow rapidly and put on lots of weight as they move closer to ten weeks of age. Soon the bunnies will become big bunnies that are capable of surviving without their mother or litter mates. Thus begins a new cycle of the bunnies' lives...

Facts about Kindling and Birthing Bunnies

- Generally it takes 30 days for a doe to produce a litter of bunnies
- A large rabbit's average litter size consists of around 6 to 8 kits
- Bunnies are born furless with their eyes closed
- Kits open their eyes at around 9 to 11 days of age
- Baby bunnies are normally birthed inside of a nest box
- Bunnies are dependent upon mother's milk until at least four weeks of age
- A mother rabbit will generally feed her kits twice a day
- Rabbits under age three will generally produce the largest litters of bunnies
- Mother rabbits will often give birth to their bunnies in the evening or in the early morning
- Smaller rabbit breeds tend to produce smaller litter sizes
- It takes about a week for newborn bunnies to develop a full coat of fur

Preparing for Kindling

Although rabbits are quite independent creatures you will still need to perform a few tasks to help your does get ready to give birth. I usually begin preparing for kits 27 days after breeding my does. Although different breeders have different systems, here is a list of things that I do to help my does get ready to deliver bunnies...

The Nest Box

The most important thing that you will need to do for your does is to get them a nest box and place it in their cage. Your does will give birth to kits inside the nest box, which is also referred to as a "bunny box" or "kindling box". I place a nest box inside of my does' cages 27 days after the first breeding. Some breeders will place the nest box in their cages up to a week before they expect bunnies, to give their does extra time to prepare. The gesture is nice however in my opinion this just allows for more time for the nest box to get dirty.

Types of Nest Boxes

There are two different types of nest boxes; wooden nest boxes and metal nest boxes. Wooden nest boxes are easy and cheap to build and serve as a great tool to help keep your bunnies warm in the winter. The one downfall of wooden nest boxes is the fact that they are harder to clean out and deodorize. Metal nest boxes on the other hand are easier to clean and are a better solution for keeping bunnies cool in the summer. I personally choose to use wooden nest boxes and construct my own. (For recommended nest box dimensions and building instructions check out the next section of this book; Build Rabbit Housing)

Nesting Material

You will need to provide your does with some type of nesting material for them to build their nest with. I simply place several full handfuls of grass hay into my rabbits' cages on the same day that I set the nest boxes into their cages. Some breeders choose to place the hay into the nest box when they place it inside of a doe's cage. I choose to just set the hay into the cages outside of the nest boxes so my does are free to build their own nests. This way I can tell whether or not a doe is going to deliver bunnies. If a doe picks up the hay with her mouth and pushes it into her nest box it is almost guaranteed that she will deliver bunnies within the next few days.

Quick Tip: Some breeders choose to place odor absorbent wood shavings into their does nest boxes instead of using hay.

Breeding to Kindling and Beyond

Here is a step by step overview of the cycle between breeding, kindling and beyond…

Step 1: Before your breed you does it is important to develop a rabbit breeding plan. Decide which does you plan on breeding to which bucks and then determine the purpose for the breeding.

Step 2: Once you have came up with a basic breeding plan, begin taking your does to the buck's cage to begin the mating process.

Step 3: Record the mating. Remember that a rabbit's gestation cycle takes approximately 30 days.

Step 4: If you wish you can try to palpate your does after approximately 14 days of pregnancy. This way if any of your does aren't pregnant then you can try to breed them again.

Step 5: Approximately 27 days after mating your does, begin to distribute out nest boxes. Also be sure to place some type of nesting material in your does' cages. I recommend using grass hay.

Step 6: Your does should begin moving the nesting material inside their nest boxes and begin building a nest. If they don't do anything with the material there is unfortunately a good chance that they are not pregnant.

Step 7: If your does are indeed pregnant they will usually deliver their bunnies 30 days after being bred. Sometimes the gestation cycle may be a couple days longer or shorter, so don't get too impatient.

Step 8: Once a doe has delivered her bunnies she will pull fur from her chest and begin building a nest on top of her bunnies. Normally weather and temperature will determine just how big she makes her nest.

Step 9: Each day if everything goes right, your does will hop inside of their nest boxes and feed their kits. Normally does will only feed their kits twice a day, once in the morning and once in the evening.

Quick Tip: I suggest that you take your does' nest boxes out of their cages periodically to make sure that all the kits are doing well and to dispose of any waste material or deceased kits. You can also consider fostering bunnies from huge litters to smaller litters in order to help even out your does' workload.

Step 10: Once your kits reach one week of age they will have acquired their first coat of fur. At this time it is safe to frequently pick up your bunnies.

Step 11: At about 10 days of age your bunnies should begin to open their eyes. If the bunnies don't all open their eyes within the next few days I suggest that you attempt to open their eyes for them. To open their eyes all you need to do is take the bunny out of its nest box, and then get a damp paper towel and gently pull its eyelid open. Doing this is important due to the fact that rabbits can acquire an eye infection if they don't open their eyes soon enough.

Step 12: I would suggest keeping your does' nest boxes in their cages until your bunnies reach three weeks of age. By this time your bunnies should have begun to hop out of their nest box.

Step 13: Once your bunnies reach approximately four weeks of age they should be eating a good deal of their mother's grain. At about this time you can begin to dramatically increase the feed of your does' that have litters of bunnies to feed. Some breeders will actually wean their bunnies at four weeks of age, however, I suggest that you at least wait until week six.

Step 14: When you feel that your bunny rabbits are big enough it is a good idea to go ahead and tattoo them while they are still young. I personally will go ahead and tattoo every single bunny no matter the circumstance.

Step 15: Once you have reached this point you are essentially done with the baby bunny phase and ready to move on to managing and dealing with your increased rabbit population. It is still important that you continue to monitor the feed, health and growth of your bunnies as they move closer to market age.

Kindling and Birthing Problems

Over the years I have received quite a few urgent phone calls at around 10:00 P.M. from rabbit raisers who are having rabbit kindling complications. Hopefully in this article I will clear up some of the "haze" and present you with some useful information...

Problem #1: My doe just had her bunnies on the cage wire!

First off this is unfortunately a pretty common situation that you can't do a whole lot about. Approximately once every couple months during breeding season I will have a doe give birth to bunnies on the cage wire instead of inside of a nest box. Sometimes this circumstance could be a consequence for incorrectly sexing a rabbit, however most the time it is simply a mistake on a doe's part. One time I was walking into my barn when I saw a bunch of new born kits crawling all over the floor under an "all doe" cage. Apparently I had incorrectly sexed one of the rabbits as being a doe instead of a buck. (OOPS) Normally does that have their bunnies on the wire are first time inexperienced mothers. If a doe has her bunnies on the wire more than once while there is a nest box in her cage I suggest getting rid of the doe. Most of the time, when a rabbit gives birth to their bunnies on the wire they will be dead before you find them. If they are still alive when you find them, you can try and save them by fostering them to another doe.

Quick Tip: Normally when a doe delivers her bunnies on the cage wire she will not take care of them even if you do decide to place them inside of her nest box. For this reason I highly recommend fostering the bunnies if possible.

Problem #2: Help, my doe is eating her bunnies!

As tragic as this circumstance may sound, your doe is most likely eating her bunnies due to inherited instinct. Here is a list of reasons why your doe might be eating her kits...

1. Your doe senses danger in the area and naturally wants to hide her nest from predators. (try to keep any potential predators such as dogs and cats away from your rabbits, especially when they have just given birth)
2. Something is wrong with the bunnies that she is eating. (believe it or not, does can actually tell when a bunny has a disease or sickness and they naturally will try to get the contaminated kit away from the rest of the bunnies)
3. Your doe might not have enough protein in her diet. (One of the survival instincts of your doe might be eating its young if she isn't getting enough protein in her diet. I feed all my does an 18% feed to prevent this problem)

4. One of the bunnies may have died and the doe is just cleaning it up. The doe's instincts tell her that having dead carcasses around will not only attract predators it will also attract bacteria and rodents.

Although cannibalism sounds horrible to us, you have to understand that from the doe's point of view it is necessary to survival. Although in captivity the dangers of the wild are most likely gone, the rabbits' internal instincts tell them differently.

There are several things that you can do to help prevent this issue from happening in the first place…

- Clean out nest boxes frequently and remove any dead bunnies
- Make sure your does have their bunnies in a quiet and low stress environment
- Feed your does a high protein feed and make sure that they are getting enough to eat
- Get rid of does that consistently cannibalize kits

Problem #3: My doe had her bunnies but didn't pull any fur!

If you experience this problem the first thing you should do is take into consideration the weather. If it is warm enough outside as long as your doe feeds her kits everything should be ok. If it is cold outside you definitely will have a problem. I would suggest trying to pull out some fur from the doe's chest to build a nest for her. It should be fairly easy since she just had her bunnies and should have pulled it out herself. I personally keep a couple of spare bags of rabbit fur on hand that I collect during rabbit molting season, just in case I have a rabbit doe that doesn't pull fur. Alternatively you could try and just foster the bunnies to another doe. (see the next page of this book for fostering information)

Problem #4: My doe only had one bunny!

Sometimes rabbits do have extremely small litters. This usually happens as a result of a doe being bred in poor condition. Sometimes however this circumstance is simply an indicator that your doe will deliver more bunnies within the next few days. I have had this circumstance take place in my rabbitry multiple times. One day a doe has a single kit, the next day she delivers six, seven or even ten more.

Summary Tip: Generally a good rule of thumb when breeding does is to give them three strikes. If they don't successfully raise up a litter of bunnies after the third breeding they should be gotten rid of, unless they are a beloved pet.

Additional Kindling and Bunny Growing Advice

Although the last few pages have more than covered the basics to kindling and growing bunnies I thought I would throw in an additional couple pages of rabbit kindling and growing advice to help you out...

Rabbit Wives Tales

There are several myths about rabbit raising that seem to originate from nothing but old wives tales. Some of the most popular myths regard baby rabbits. Supposedly many people believe that if you mess with a doe's kits too early she will stop taking care of them. I personally have never had this issue in all the years that I have raised rabbits. Normally I will pull the nest box from a doe's cage a couple days after she has delivered bunnies and clean out any waste materials that happen to be inside the nest box. So in my opinion it doesn't matter if you mess with your bunnies, the mother rabbit will still take care of them.

Quick Tip: There is a good chance that this myth could have originated with regard to wild rabbits not domestic rabbits. So it is still a good idea to not mess with any bunnies that you happen to find in the wild.

Fostering:

Another of the popular rabbit wives tales involves fostering bunnies. Many non-rabbit raisers hold the belief that it is a dangerous move to try and foster bunnies. Supposedly these people believe that a doe will try and get rid of any kits in her nest box that are not her own. From my experience I have found that normally a doe won't be able to tell whether a bunny is hers or not, either she doesn't realize or flat out doesn't care. I commonly foster bunnies from larger litters to smaller litters. This is one of the reasons that I recommend breeding multiple does during the same time period. Many times fostering bunnies will help save lives that would otherwise be lost. In the winter when the temperatures are at or below freezing, fostering is highly important. For instance if a doe only has two bunnies there most likely won't be enough body heat within the nest box to keep both the bunnies warm enough. In this case I would suggest fostering a few more bunnies into the litter to help keep the two alive. Also, if you have too many bunnies in a litter they will have a hard time surviving during cold weather. So I would take a few bunnies away from the larger litter and give them to a mother with fewer kits.

Quick Tip: The ideal number of bunnies per litter is about 6. Example: If one of your does has ten bunnies and another only has two; I would suggest moving four bunnies into the nest box with only two kits.

Quick Tip #2: One other thing that I want to point out is the fact that does that have already birthed litters will tend to take better care of their bunnies than first time mothers. So keep this in mind when making fostering decisions.

Tracking Fostered Bunnies

One of the main problems with fostering bunnies is the fact that you will have a much harder time figuring out which bunnies belong to which parents. This can definitely create complications when you are trying to keep pedigree records on all of your rabbits. You will most likely be left wondering if your guesswork was indeed accurate. One rabbit breeder that I know came up with a nice little solution to solving this problem. When they foster bunnies they tattoo a tiny tattoo character into the bunnies' ears. This way they can for sure tell which bunnies belong to which does. Another way to keep track of bunnies when fostering is to mark them with a permanent marker. Unfortunately the mother rabbit will generally try to lick the marker off of the bunnies. One breeder that I know resorted to putting a long marker stripe down each of the bunnies' backs (at this point they were still furless so the marker wouldn't stain their coat). Each day he would take the fostered bunnies out of the nest box and put a new stripe on each of their backs. Although this solution works I by far prefer the small tattoo based method.

Fostering Bunnies – Won't the Mother Get Upset?

People often tell me that they don't want to foster bunnies due to the fact that they do not want to upset the mother rabbit. A friend of mine once made a very truthful statement; "Mother rabbits can't count". A doe knows that she has bunnies but since she can't count she will not get upset when bunnies are fostered out of her nest box! Read that statement again. ☺

To Wean or Not to Wean – Should I wean my rabbits?

This is the type of question that if you ask five people you will most likely get eight different opinions. ☺ If you are raising up bunnies for show this is a very important decision. I personally don't recommend weaning bunnies before about week eight unless you need to. Basically one thing I need to point out though is the fact that bunnies often lose condition when they are first weaned. So I wouldn't recommend weaning bunnies right before a show.

Build Rabbit Housing

Choosing to build your own rabbit housing can help save you lots of money in the long run. One of the main advantages of building your own housing and supplies is the fact that you can build to fit your custom needs instead of having to make do with what you can buy. However if you are not able or willing to dedicate a decent amount of time to building rabbit housing supplies, I strongly advise you to skip this section and buy your rabbit supplies instead. Constructing supplies can be fairly simple if you follow my advice however this is not an endeavor that the "faint in heart" should attempt.

Items that you can build yourself
- Rabbit Cages
- Hutches
- Sheds/Buildings
- Nest Boxes
- Hay Feeder

> Automatic Rabbit Watering System:
> **RabbitBreeders.us/AutoWater**
> -Check out the link above for the exact plan that I used to setup my automatic watering system.

Nest Boxes: See page 73

Hay Rack: See page 79

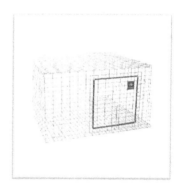

All Wire Cage: See page 77

Decide to Buy Instead? – Check out the following store link...

Premium Rabbit Supplies: http://PremiumRabbits.com/

Building a Rabbit Barn

Here is a list of resources that you might find useful when attempting to build your own rabbit barn or shed…

Free Rabbit Barn Plans:

Rabbit Barn Layout: http://rabbitbreeders.us/BarnLayout6340

Cage/Barn Arrangement Plans: http://rabbitbreeders.us/ArrangementPlans

Rabbit Hutch w/ Cover: http://rabbitbreeders.us/Hutch6277

Building a Barn:

Step by Step Guide to Building a Pole Barn: http://www.pole-barn.info/how-to-build-pole-barn.html

Barn Design Plans/Ideas: http://www.barnsbarnsbarns.com/

Agricultural Facility Plans: http://rabbitbreeders.us/AgriculturalFacilityPlans

My Barn:

A few years back one of my family members who has a talent for building low cost quality facilities, helped me construct two of my current 32 ft long by 14 ft wide rabbit buildings. Hopefully you can figure out how to copy the basic design from looking at the pictures below…

Good Luck!

How to Construct a Rabbit Nest Box

Most rabbit breeders would agree on the fact that nest boxes are essential kindling supplies that any rabbit raiser should obtain if they plan on breeding their does. Nest boxes help keep your new born bunnies safe and warm in addition to giving your doe a sense of security. If you have multiple does it can get expensive to have to buy all your nest boxes, so here is a step by step tutorial on how to construct your own rabbit nest box.

Step 1: Decide on a Model: There are several different nest box models that you can choose to build. The main nest box models include; Wooden Nest Boxes, Wood and Wire Nest Boxes and All Metal Nest Boxes. There are then several different types of each of these models that come in all different sizes and dimensions. See pictures listed below for a visual image...

Nest Box 1: Metal Nest Box

Nest Box 2: Open Wood and Wire Nest Box

Nest Box 3: Open Wood Nest Box w/ Wire Bottom

Nest Box 4: Wooden Enclosed Nest Box

Remember some rabbit breeders prefer different models for different reasons, so you are free to choose which model you like best. I personally prefer using the Wooden Enclosed Nest Box.

Note: For the purpose of this tutorial I am going to teach you how to construct a wooden enclosed nest box (**Nest Box 4**) because that is the type I have successfully used for years.

Step 2: Buy Materials: The first step to constructing wooden enclosed nest boxes is to go purchase several sheets of plywood which will be used to build the nest box frame. One of the best things about wooden nest boxes is the fact that they are cheap and easy to make.

Note: the plywood that I use is approximately ½ inch thick

Step 3: Cut Plywood: To start out the building process I will make six rectangles out of plywood sheets. I cut out the following dimensions…

2 Sides: 19 in. wide by 13 in. tall
Front: 14 in. wide by 13 in. tall
Back: 13 in. wide by 12.5 in. tall
Bottom: 19 in. long by 13 in. wide
Top: 19.5 in. long by 14 in. wide

Step 4: Cutout Opening: You will need cutout a section of the "Front" board so that your rabbit can access the nest box. I recommend that you draw a line down the middle of the width of the board and then divide the board into four quadrants. Now cut out either the upper left or right quadrant of the board.

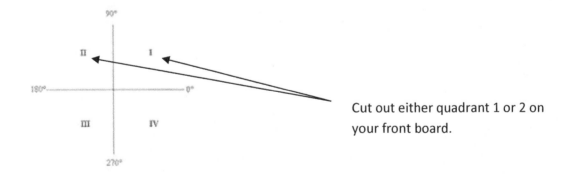

Cut out either quadrant 1 or 2 on your front board.

Step 5: Now use small nails to nail the bottom board to the front board (make sure the cutout in the board is facing the top) and then go around clockwise nailing the other boards (excluding the top piece) in place. The back board should sit on top of the bottom board so that the height is even with the sides.

Step 6: If everything went smoothly you should now have your whole nest box created except for the top. Next I will set my top board to rest on top of the other boards and make sure that it is aligned properly. Then I will get a screw driver and drill four holes in the sides of the top board. Ideally I want the holes in the top board to be a tad bit larger than the screws so that I can lift the board off the top of the screws with a little effort. (I am doing this with the holes so that I can create a lid for my nest box)

Step 7: Now finish drilling the screws into the sides of the board. You want the screws to stay in place in the sides of the boards so don't expand the holes like you did to the top board.

Hopefully by now you should have a nest box that looks similar to the one shown below! (Minus the hay of course)

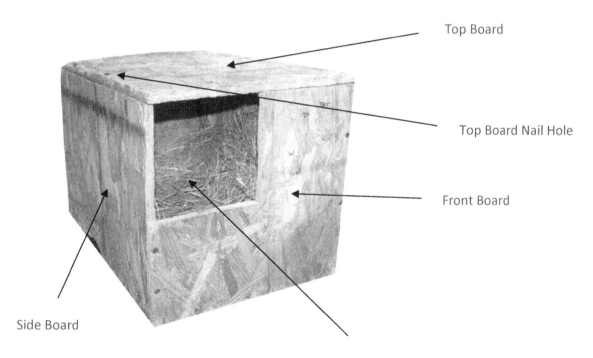

- Top Board
- Top Board Nail Hole
- Front Board
- Side Board
- Upper Left Quadrant Board Opening

Alternative Nest Box Design Plan

Here is an image design plan of a nest box that you can construct that has wooden sides, an open top and a wire bottom...

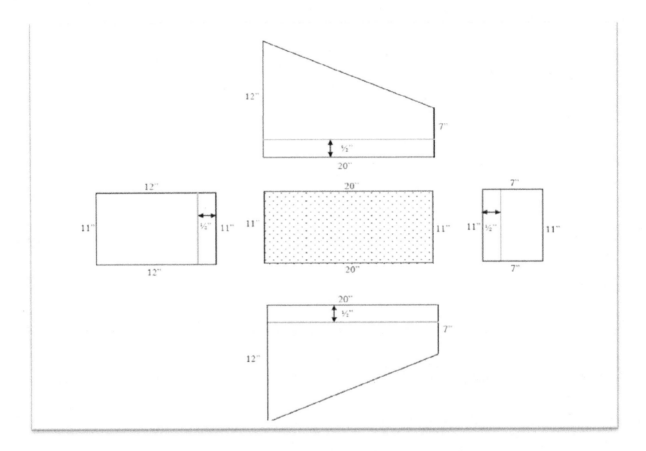

Note: If you wish you can partially enclose the top by attaching another board with a hole in it. For this design however I recommend simply keeping the top open.

You can also choose to make the bottom of wood however I recommend using wire due to the fact that it will allow urine and other wastes to leave the nest box.

Good Luck Designing your Nest Boxes!

Quick Tip: If you get good enough at designing nest boxes you can potentially make and sell them to local breeders in your area for a cheaper price than they would have pay in a regular supply store.

How to Build a Rabbit Cage

One of the most expensive items that people purchase for their rabbits is a rabbit cage. Here is a step by step tutorial on how to build your own rabbit cage with the purpose of saving money...

Step 1: Decide on a Cage Type and Material: I recommend making all wire cages for multiple reasons including; the fact that they are easy to clean, easier to move around, last longer and can even be cheaper to make than the traditional wood and wire cages. Below are several rabbit cage and hutch pictures that can help aid you in your decision...

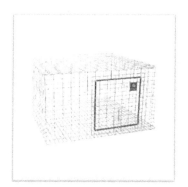  

Note: For the purpose of this article I am going to be showing you how to build a typical all wire rabbit cage. If you are looking for additional rabbit cage designs and plans check out the links below... (the links below are to free reports that you can download that have been produced by reputable organizations such as universities and colleges)

Main Recommended Rabbit Housing Manual:
http://rabbitbreeders.us/rabbithousingmanualpdf

Home Made Rabbit Cages: http://rabbitbreeders.us/HomeMadeRabbitCages
4 Rowed Rabbit Cage Plans: http://rabbitbreeders.us/4RowedCagePlans
6 Rowed Rabbit Cage Plans: http://rabbitbreeders.us/6RowedCagePlans

Rabbit Housing Plans: http://rabbitbreeders.us/PSUHousingPlans

Step 2: Gather your Supplies: Here is a list of supplies and equipment that you will need to build the all wire rabbit cage
- Hammer
- Wire Cutters

- J-Clip Pliers
- J-clips
- Wooden 2 x 4 (2-ft. long)
- Measure tape or yard stick

Wire:
- Sides: 1 length 1-in x 2-in, 14 gauge galvanized wire fencing
  Dimensions: 18 in. wide by 11 ft. long
- Bottom: 1 piece ½-in. x 1-in, 14 gauge welded wire
  Dimensions: 30 in. by 36 in.
- Top: 1 piece 1 in by 2 in., 14 gauge galvanized wire mesh
  Dimensions: 30 in. by 36 in.
- Door: 1 piece 1 in. by 2 in., 14 gauge galvanized wire mesh
  Dimensions: Approximately 13 in. square

You can normally find wire available at your local feed or hardware store. Another great place to purchase cage wire is at Lowe's.

Step 3: Begin Building: Lay the side wire piece on the ground and grab the wooden 2 by 4 and your hammer. Next using your hammer try to bend the wire around the corner of the wooden 2 by 4 to create the two 3 foot and 2 ½ foot sides.

Step 4: Finish the Sides: Once you have bent the wire start fastening the rectangle in place by clamping the J-clips on with your J-clip pliers. You should attach a clip about every 3 inches on the side.

Step 5: Attach the Bottom: Next attach the ½ in. by 1 in. mesh wire piece to the sides you just created with J-clips and pliers to make the bottom.

Step 6: Attach the Top: In the same way that you attached the bottom attach the 1 in. by 2 in. mesh wire piece to form the top of the cage.

Step 7: Build the Door: Using your pair of wire clippers cut an opening 1 foot square on the wide side of the wire. Be sure to leave approximately ½ inch stubs on the cut wire. Next do your best to bend the wire stubs back with the clippers so that the edges are smooth and attach the door wire piece.

Note: The door should overlap the other wire at least ½ inch all the way around.

How to Build a Hay Feeder

Building a rabbit hay feeder is quite frankly a very simple task. All you will need is a few minutes and some rabbit cage wire. Here are some step by step instructions on how to assemble one...

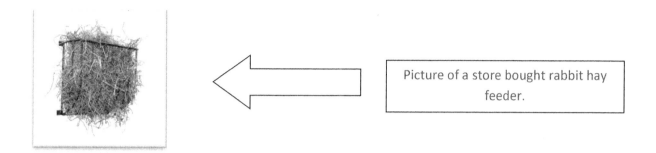

Picture of a store bought rabbit hay feeder.

Step 1: Decide on a Cage Location: Pick a spot on your rabbit's cage where you would like a hay feeder to hang. Keep in mind that the hay rack should not hang on the door of the cage or next to your rabbit's water bottle.

Step 2: Gather your Materials: You will need to get out your pair of gloves and wire clippers to cutout the wire for the hay rack. The wire cutting should be around 6 inches wide and 8 inches long.

Step 3: Start Constructing: Next take the piece of wire and bend its two opposite sides into a rectangular U shape. Try to make one side slightly higher than the other and be sure to leave an opening at the top and on the sides.

Step 4: Pay Attention to Details: Be sure to clip off any sharp edges on your hay rack to ensure the safety of your rabbit that is bound to rub its chin against the structure.

Step 5: Attach the Rack: Now it is time to attach the new hay rack to your rabbit's cage... Attach the hay rack to one of the sides of your rabbit's cage using a leash clip. Be sure that the hay rack is secure in its new location.

Step 6: Collect the Dust: If you have your rabbit cages indoors it is recommended that you place a piece of plastic under the hay rack to catch any dust that might fall through.

Quick Tip: I recommend making all of your rabbits hay feeders to make it easier to feed them hay. Ideally if you have quite a few rabbits; you will build a hay feeder that multiple rabbits have access to.

Part 3: Rabbit Herd Management and Stock Evaluation

How to Sex a Rabbit

Every rabbit raiser needs to know how to accurately sex a rabbit. Below I have included a set of step by step instructions on how to sex a rabbit...

Step 1: Bring the rabbit that you wish to sex to a flat surface such as a rabbit judging table.

Step 2: Next carefully grab a hold of the rabbit's tail and lift it upwards so that the rabbit's back feet are off the ground. Note: Some people recommend cradling the rabbit in your arm instead.

Step 3: Use your forefinger and middle finger to press down on your rabbit's vent area which is just in front of the anus. If the rabbit is a buck the penis should protrude. If the rabbit is a doe you should see a slit or central line running up and down. See the picture below...

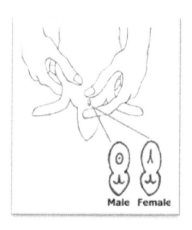
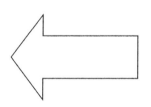

Quick Tip:
If you are having trouble sexing a rabbit on your own, try to find a local rabbit breeder who would be willing to help teach you hands on.

When Sexing is Easy

Once a buck reaches several months of age you should be able to tell that he is a buck by just glancing due to the fact that his testicles will begin to protrude.

Believe it or not I can tell the sex of a full grown rabbit by simply glancing at its head and chin! Once you have seen enough rabbits you should be able to do the same. The easiest way to tell that a rabbit is a doe is by looking at its chin. Does naturally develop dewlaps (fat rolls) under their chin to store up fat. When a doe has bunnies her dewlap will usually shrink.

When Sexing is Hard

Unfortunately when bunnies are really small it can be hard to tell whether a rabbit is a doe or a buck. From time to time you are bound to make a sexing error, even I do sometimes.

Parts of a Rabbit Chart

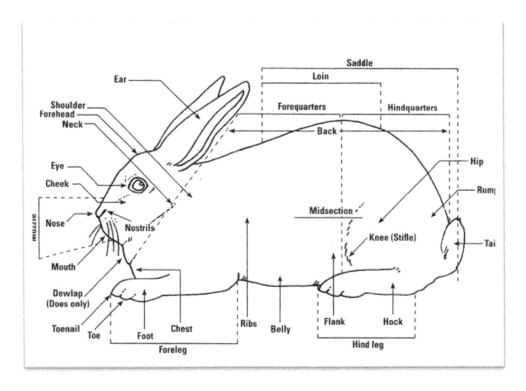

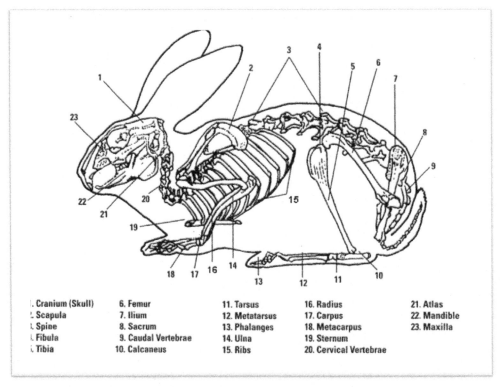

1. Cranium (Skull)	6. Femur	11. Tarsus	16. Radius	21. Atlas
2. Scapula	7. Ilium	12. Metatarsus	17. Carpus	22. Mandible
3. Spine	8. Sacrum	13. Phalanges	18. Metacarpus	23. Maxilla
4. Fibula	9. Caudal Vertebrae	14. Ulna	19. Sternum	
5. Tibia	10. Calcaneus	15. Ribs	20. Cervical Vertebrae	

Evaluating Breeding Stock

One of the most important parts of raising rabbits is being able to evaluate breeding stock. Your ability to distinguish the good from the bad will play a key role in determining the long term success of your rabbitry. Ideally you will want to put yourself in a position where you are able to pick out the best animals from a litter to either keep or sell to others. As most reputable rabbit breeders will tell you, evaluating stock takes a ton of practice and patience. A friend of mine once said that "After feeling your first thousand rabbits you tend to get the hang of what you are doing". If you are new to the rabbit world this statement can seem discouraging however I urge you to continue. Below is some information which should be able to help you out…

Qualities of a Great Breeding Stock Rabbit
- Grows faster than the rest of the bunnies born in the litter
- Remains healthy and requires very little treatment
- Stays in good condition during harsh weather either too cold or too hot
- Willingly breeds
- Produces large litters of quality offspring
- Has a good body type

What is a Good Body Type?

Before we go any further I want to take a minute to expand on the last bullet point. Regardless of whether you are breeding for meat, pets, show animals or for fur quality I believe it is important to keep nice big healthy animals. I want these animals to have broad shoulders, a good loin, and good hindquarters. If you are raising one of the more fancy breeds of rabbits you should put more emphasis on markings and fur. Animals that exhibit these traits are bound to be your best producers due to the fact that they tend to carry the most desirable dominant genes. A little small rabbit might make a nice pet for someone however to produce that rabbit I would want to use quality breeding stock that exhibits superiority over the rest of my herd. From all my years of testing things out, I clearly have seen a pattern in offspring health. **Large healthy parents tend to produce healthy offspring**. Read that statement one more time please.

The Doe vs the Buck

Well obviously you will want to look for different desirable traits in your bucks than in your does. When keeping a doe I ideally want the doe to have a good body type in addition to good mothering abilities. I want my bucks to be big, bulky and be willingly to breed all the time.

Rabbit Identification

Once you begin to acquire a large herd of rabbits you will need to come up with a workable system for identifying your rabbits. I recommend that you come up with and implement this system from day one, however that is totally your choice and not mine...

A question that many first time rabbit raisers always ask me is, "how can I tell all my rabbits apart from each other?"

Answer: You need to tattoo them! As of now there is simply no other way to as effectively and efficiently tell rabbits apart than the classic rabbit ear tattoo. I recommend that you tattoo all your rabbits to avoid potential confusion... Just picture for a moment, several of your rabbits happen to get loose out of their cages and you realize that you can't tell them apart. Note: I have had to learn the hard way on this recommendation.

Rabbit Tattooing Systems

So now that you realize the importance of tattooing your rabbits it is time for me to discuss rabbit tattooing systems. Ideally when you look at your rabbit's tattoo you will not only want to be able to identify the rabbit, you will also want to be able to "know something about the rabbit". Some breeders wish to know the month and year in which the rabbit was born, just by looking at its ear tattoo. Others breeders choose to use a more complex system so that they are able to tell just how many bunnies were born in the litter or the number of bucks and does that "popped out" from the breeding.

Date Method: One way that you can perform this method is by using just numbers. For instance you can tattoo a four digit number into you rabbits' ears. The first two numbers can be the month they were born and the last two can be the year. Example: Using this method if I had a rabbit born in March 2009 their tattoo would be; 0309. The only problem with this system is the fact that you will be giving multiple rabbits the same tattoo. So I recommend adding an extra letter and number to the tattoo. You could start with A1 for example and continue tattooing the rabbits until you reach A9 and then start on B1 and keep going down the alphabet. Example: The third rabbit that you tattoo that was born in March 2009 would have the tattoo; A30309.

My Method: Here is a method that I personally developed which seems to work great... First assign each of your does and bucks which have bunnies a letter from A to Z (excluding x). Personally I give each of my rabbits who have had kits their own name and use that letter.

(Check out the bonus section of this book for a huge rabbit names idea list!) Now when you tattoo a rabbit you will place the rabbit's mother's letter first followed by its father's. To give the rabbit a unique identity you can place a number before the letters. For Example: If I had a kit born to my A doe and T buck its tattoo would be a number followed by the letters AT. If the rabbit was the first that I tattooed its tattoo would be 1AT. Additionally I weigh my bunnies from each litter before I tattoo them and start the tattooing process with the heaviest rabbit on down to the least heavy rabbit. This way I can tell three things by just looking at the three or four digit tattoo; the rabbit's father, mother and its weight position in comparison to the rest of the litter at the time of the tattooing! I have found over the years that the heaviest bunnies at tattooing age are usually going to be the "premium of the litter". So based upon theory; I would expect the lower numbers in each litter to grow up to be the better rabbits. Now one more thing regarding the X... if you are like me you may eventually acquire more than 26 breeding does during a given period, so to solve this issue I will create a second alphabet using each letter followed by X. For example: if I had two does with the letter A, I would assign the second one an AX instead of just a pure A. So if I bred the second doe to the T buck her kits would have the letters; AXT.

How to Tattoo a Rabbit

Here are some step by step instructions on how to properly tattoo one of your rabbits...

Step 1: Order the Supplies- Depending upon your rabbit tattoo system you may need to order a tattooing kit that comes with multiple sets of alphabetic and numerical characters. You will also need to order rabbit tattooing ink unless the kit that you purchase comes with some. Additionally you will need a box of Q tips which will be used during the tattooing process. If you don't have any on hand click here to order some.

Looking to get a Rabbit Tattooing Kit? You can buy one via: http://PremiumRabbits.com/

Quick Tip: I recommend using India ink for your tattooing needs, the stuff seems to work better and is much cheaper than the ink labeled specifically for rabbit tattooing.

Step 2: Decide on a Tattooing System- I recommend that you either use one of the tattooing systems recommended above or modify one of them to fit your identification desires.

Step 3: Pick a Location and Arrange Supplies- Find a flat table location that you feel would be appropriate for tattooing rabbits. I recommend laying a piece of carpet on the table so that your rabbits won't be sliding around while you are trying to tattoo them. Place your rabbit tattoo kit on the table along with the box of Q tips. Also be sure to have some wet paper towels on hand. Lastly bring the rabbit that you wish to tattoo to the table.

Step 4: Tattoo the Rabbit- Once you have arranged your supplies and placed the tattoo characters into the clamp you can begin the tattooing process. (Be sure to rub ink on the characters) Take the rabbit's left ear with your non dominant hand and then center the clamp in the middle of your rabbit's ear. Count to three in your head and then give the clamp a good squeeze. The rabbit may squeal for a second or two however they will calm down shortly. Now take a Q tip and rub some more ink into the imprint that is hopefully showing in the rabbit's ear. Don't be alarmed if ink bleeds out on the other side of the ear, in fact some rabbit breeders claim this is the #1 sign of a "successful tattoo". If you accidently hit one of the rabbit's blood veins while tattooing, the ear may bleed a bit.

Quick Tip: Tattoo your rabbits when they are bunnies. Their ears are softer then and tattooing will be easier. Also as your rabbits' ears grow the tattoo will expand.

Quick Tip #2: If your rabbit's ears bleed apply some Terramycin onto the spot.

Looking to Purchase Rabbit Tattooing Supplies? Check out the following link:

Premium Rabbit Supplies: http://PremiumRabbits.com/

Pedigrees 101

If you plan on selling rabbit breeding stock or show rabbits it is essential that you try your best to keep up with pedigree information. Many rabbit raisers will refuse to buy a rabbit if it doesn't come with a pedigree. Luckily pedigree information is much easier to keep up with than it was a decade ago due to invention of rabbit pedigree software. In the old days breeders would have to handwrite out pedigrees on their rabbits, now there are several software programs available which allow you to produce pedigrees in seconds.

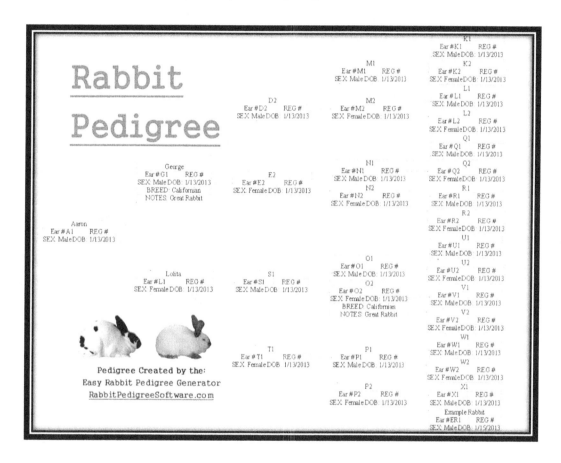

Recommended Rabbit Software:

Not only do some of these software programs allow you to create pedigrees they also help you manage your rabbitry. Here is a short list of the software programs that I recommend...

- The Easy Rabbit Pedigree Software: http://RabbitPedigreeSoftware.com/
- The Easy Rabbitry Management Software: http://RabbitryManagementSoftware.com/

Record Keeping

Whether you like it or not it is extremely important to keep good rabbitry records. Even if you have the best memory in the world from time to time you will forget things. This is especially true if you are like me and have a habit of keeping a ton of rabbits. There is no way on god's green earth that you can possibly keep track of everything in your head when you raise hundreds of rabbits. (Unless you're the Einstein of record keeping)

In my opinion there are four main types of rabbitry records that you need to keep:
- Breeding Records
- Finance Records
- Kindling/Birthing Records
- Individual Rabbit Records (includes pedigrees)

I recommend that you keep your records in a spiral notebook or digitally on the computer. I personally use a piece of rabbitry software titled The Easy Rabbitry Management Software available via: http://RabbitryManagementSoftware.com/ for record keeping purposes.

Please be sure to frequently backup your data... I know this might seem like common sense to you, (like it did to me when I got started) however please don't learn the hard way like I did! To make a long story short; my house got robbed, my computer was stolen and a huge amount of my rabbit data was permanently lost! It was one of the worst days of my life when I found out that hundreds of my rabbit records and pedigrees that I had spent a huge amount of time creating were permanently gone.):

Rabbit Hutch Cards

Quite a few breeders that I know use rabbit hutch cards to help keep track of their herd. The hutch cards might contain information about the animal in the cage such as date of birth, sex, awards, breeding and kindling information, etc...

Recently I have heard about a rabbit breeder who keeps rabbit hutch records using a magnet system. The breeder uses magnets to help organize their rabbitry and to mark which cages contain bucks and does. You can also use magnets to mark cages that you need to clean out or cages in which you need to insert nest boxes into.

Just be creative, the possibilities are literally endless!!

Blueprints for Growing and Expanding your Herd

Stock Management/Estimated Production Chart

# of Breeder Rabbits	# of Does	# of Bucks	Kits Produced Annually
<u>3</u>	2	1	36-72
<u>5</u>	3	2	90-180
<u>10</u>	8	2	180-360
<u>20</u>	17	3	360-720
<u>30</u>	26	4	540-1080
<u>50</u>	45	5	900-1800
<u>100</u>	95	5	1800-3600
<u>250</u>	240	10	4500-9000
<u>1,000</u>	970	30	18000-36000

Rabbitry Color Codes		
Small/Hobby	Intermediate	Commercial

Variables	
Number of Rabbits Born/Litter	6
Number of Breedings/Year	3 and 6

Note: This chart predicts the average number of kits based upon experimental data. This data is based upon the average production rate of a healthy rabbit in the large breed category such as the Californian or New Zealand. This data has been produced to supply a visual estimate only. Results and production will vary based upon your individual animals and by breed.

Chart Explanation/Notes:

I typed the chart up on the last page with the purpose of helping rabbit raisers estimate herd production and expand their rabbitries. Although the chart is fairly simple I wish I would have been given a copy when I first started raising rabbits. Many rabbit raisers struggle with managing a growing rabbit herd. When I first started out I was one of those struggling rabbit raisers. I found myself with too many rabbits even though I was anxious to expand… If I would have been able to take a look at the color coded chart I believe I would have been able to figure out what one of my main problems was… I simply had too many bucks! At that time I had a small/hobby rabbitry consisting of eight does and five bucks. So the extra three bucks were complicating things by taking up space in my already crowded small shed that I had at the time. I ended up sacrificing giving my best animals their own cages by giving the "extra 3" bucks the cages instead! My advice is this… if you keep 10 or fewer breeding does do NOT keep more than three bucks. If you have bucks that don't breed very well I recommend replacing them, unless you have a special reason to keep them. Also if you have too many bucks you will find it harder to keep up with pedigree information.

The Decreasing Buck to Doe Ratio

As your herd expands your buck to doe ratio of your "breeding animals" should decrease. Example: I recommend that if you only have five breeding rabbits, you keep two bucks. I recommend that you keep two bucks due to the fact that it is always important to have a backup. If you have 8 does you still only need two bucks due to the fact that two decent bucks can pretty easily keep eight does bred. I had a buck once that literally bred over a hundred times within a three day period! (LOL I know; he was one of my best) Also, if you have a large commercial herd you will generally develop an efficient breeding cycle so that you constantly are having bunnies born. This way the bucks won't have to breed all the does at once.

Annual Kit Production + X

Although it would have been too difficult to try and display on the chart; I have found that if your breeding herd size doubles your kit production will more than double. For instance if you have a commercial herd consisting of 100 breeding rabbits it will be much easier to get an average of 6 kits per litter out of a doe than it would be if you only had 5 rabbits. This is normally true because as you get more animals you will have a better selection of breeding stock to choose from and can more easily get rid of non-productive animals. For instance if you had 100 breeding rabbits if you wanted to you could sell off does who only produce an average of 5 kits per litter and thus improve your herd production. So I call this the plus X factor.

Part 4: Rabbit Care Information and Advice

Rabbit Health 101

As a rabbit raiser you should place high importance upon keeping all your rabbits in good health. In this section of this book I will be discussing the different aspects of rabbit health and will be providing you with real world solutions which will hopefully help you prevent and treat illnesses that your rabbits may acquire. I hope you find the material in this section both useful and practical to your rabbit herd...

Importance of Keeping a Healthy Herd

Here is a list of reasons why you should try your best to keep a healthy rabbit herd...

- Sick herd animals will not be able to maintain their health and produce quality offspring
- Many times sick does will pass on illnesses to their offspring through direct contact
- If your rabbits are constantly getting sick, people will be very hesitant about buying rabbits from you
- Sometimes sicknesses occur in your rabbit herd due to the genetic magnification of poor quality genetics
- Sick rabbits are generally unpleasant rabbits
- Breeders who consistently keep sick rabbits will acquire a reputation of being "unethical breeders"
- Spending all your time treating sick rabbits will most likely strike a blow to the overall management process of your herd as you devote extra time to care instead of management
- Consistently treating sick rabbits will most likely put a dent in your pocketbook as you will be forced to purchase additional rabbit supplies

Preventing Diseases and Illnesses

It is much easier and time efficient to prevent your rabbits from getting sick in the first place than it is to treat illnesses. Here is a list of tips which will hopefully help you keep your rabbits healthy in the first place...

- Make sure that your rabbit building is well ventilated
- Clean your rabbit supplies on a frequent basis
- Don't let too much manure develop underneath your rabbit cages
- Avoid overcrowding your rabbits in your rabbit hutches
- Quarantine new rabbits for at least thirty days before introducing them to your herd

Signs that a Rabbit is Sick

Most of the time I am able to tell whether or not a rabbit is sick based upon several different signs and the years of rabbit care experience I have acquired. Here is a list of signs that could indicate that your rabbit is sick or has some other type of problem...

- Stops eating its food (in my opinion this is the number one indicator that something could be wrong with the rabbit)
- Quits drinking water, if you notice that a rabbit isn't drinking any water you can definitely assume that the animal is ill
- Becomes unusually inactive
- Starts acting very aggressive towards others
- Begins to shake its ears more than normal
- Develops abscesses or lumps on its skin
- Experiences common cold symptoms such as a runny nose
- Begins sneezing more than usual
- Starts losing random patches of fur (seasonal molting doesn't count)
- Discharge or puss becomes visible around the rabbit's nose
- Your rabbit consistently scratches a certain location or starts pulling out patches of fur (the act of pulling fur with the purpose of making a nest doesn't count)
- Develops a fungus somewhere on its body
- Simply starts to act strange

Rabbit Diseases and Health Problems

Here is a list of common rabbit diseases and other negative conditions that rabbits can acquire...

Bacterial Diseases:
- Abscesses
- Mastitis
- Pasteurelosis
- Pneumonia
- Sore Eyes
- Vent Disease
- Weepy Eye

Viral Diseases:
- Infectious Myxomatosis

Fungal Diseases:
- Ringworm

External Parasitic Conditions:
- Ear Mites
- Fur Mites
- Warbles

Internal Parasitic Conditions:
- Pin Worms
- Tapeworms

Non Infectious Conditions:
- Fetal Giantism
- Fur Ball
- Slobbers
- Sore Hocks
- Wet Dewlap

Health Problems: Symptoms, Causes, Treatments

Here is a chart including information on many of the most common rabbit diseases and other negative rabbit health conditions. Many of the treatments listed below have not yet been clinically accepted, only recommended by successful rabbit raisers. (Use them at your own risk)

Bacterial Diseases and Conditions			
Negative Condition	**Symptoms**	**Cause**	**Treatment**
Abscesses	Lumps may begin to appear on a rabbit's body. These lumps can literally appear anywhere however they are most commonly seen on the head, chest and belly.	Generally caused by too much trauma to a certain area. It is known that abscesses can also be caused by the spread of the bacteria Pasteurella throughout a rabbit's blood stream.	You should cut the abscess open, drain the puss and apply hydrogen peroxide on the wound daily. Some people also recommend giving your rabbit antibiotics to help treat the wound.
Mastitis	When a rabbit has Mastitis their mammary gland may appear inflamed, swollen, hot or discolored. Sometimes the rabbit will develop abscesses due to Mastitis.	Caused by a doe's over continuation of milk production after or during the weaning process. **Quick Prevention Tip:** Try weaning your kits gradually instead of all at once.	Give your rabbit a dose of injectable Penicillin G for three consecutive days. (20,000 to 40,000 IU per pound of body weight) Also try stripping the affected glands free of milk.
Pasteurelosis	Some signs that your rabbit has Pasteurelosis include; intense sneezing and white nasal discharge that is either thin or thick. This condition is also known as "Snuffles" and involves an upper respiratory infection.	This condition is caused by a bacterium known as Pasteurella multocida. **Quick Prevention Tip:** Keep your rabbits in a well ventilated area with a clean and fresh water supply	Give your rabbit some antibiotic that is recommended by a rabbit health specialist. (As far as I know there isn't any universal solution to getting rid of this infection) Move your rabbit to a clean, low stress environment and hope for the best.

Pneumonia	Signs of Pneumonia include but are not limited to; difficulty breathing, extreme tiredness and the development of bluish colored lips tongue and ears.	Pneumonia is caused by a viral or bacterial infection of the respiratory system. If your rabbit is in a high stress environment they are more likely to develop this illness.	Give your rabbit a broad-spectrum antibiotic. Additionally try to limit stress, and isolate the rabbit in order to prevent this illness from spreading to other animals in your herd.
Sore Eyes	If your rabbit's eyes are stuck shut or fail to open at about ten days of age there is a good chance that your rabbit has "sore eyes". This condition is also referred to by some breeders as "Nest Box Eye".	Sore Eyes are caused by a bacterial infection that usually develops while bunnies are inside of their nest boxes.	Remove any pus that may have developed around the rabbit's eye(s) and apply ophthalmic ointment twice a day to the sore eye. Repeat this procedure for several days to experience best results.
Vent Disease	Scabs that contain a white or yellow discharge may develop on a rabbit's nose or mouth. A scabby inflammation may also be visible on the genital area of the rabbit.	The Vent Disease is caused by the spirochete bacteria Treponema cuniculi and can be spread to other animals during the process of mating or kindling.	This condition can be treated by applying penicillin ointment to the rabbit's genital area. (20,000 to 40,000 IU per pound of body weight)
Weepy Eye	You may observe matted fur at the corner of your rabbit's eye and under the lower eyelid. Discharge may be visible on the surface of the eye and the tissue around the eye may appear irritated.	Caused by the blockage of the tear duct between the lower eyelid and the nasal area. Sometimes this condition is an after effect of a respiratory infection.	Apply ophthalmic ointment on the eye twice a day for several days or until the eye heals. If possible try to minimize stress in your rabbit's living environment.

Viral and Fungal Diseases and Conditions			
Negative Condition	Symptoms	Cause	Treatment
Myxomatosis	Symptoms of this disease vary greatly due to the fact that there are many different strands floating around. Some common symptoms include; failure to eat, high fever, inflammation of the genitals and respiratory infection.	Myxomatosis is caused by the Myxoma virus and is spread by an arthropod host such as mosquitoes, flies, gnats and fleas.	This disease is extremely deadly and there isn't any known cure. It is recommended that you try your best to keep your rabbitry free of flies, fleas and mosquitoes in order to help prevent your rabbits from catching this disease.
Ringworm	Ringworm is famous for its main symptom; loss of hair in a circular pattern with a particular sore in the middle. The most common place that Ringworm will appear on your rabbits is on their feet and legs.	Ringworm is caused and spread by contact to a certain fungus. Ringworm can be contagious and spread from rabbit to rabbit and even to humans.	Apply a daily iodine treatment to the infected area. Usually this condition isn't too serious as long as you treat the animal early on. Be sure to isolate any animals that have Ringworm.

| \multicolumn{4}{c}{**External Parasitic Conditions**} |

Negative Condition	Symptoms	Cause	Treatment
Ear Mites	One of the signs that your rabbit has Ear Mites is when you notice it constantly scratching its ears or shaking its head. When your rabbit has Ear Mites you will be able to see a yellowish scabby material inside of the rabbit's ear.	"Ear Canker" is caused by a particular mite that causes infestation within your rabbits' ears. (Psoroptes cuniculi) Ear mites love to thrive in particularly warm climates like Texas the state I live in. Ear Mites are also very contagious and will infect your entire herd unless you deal with them soon enough.	If you don't notice soon enough that your rabbit has Ear Mites they can literally kill your rabbit by making it lose its balance. The best way to treat this condition is to first clean out your rabbit's ears and then apply mineral oil onto the infected area. Another solution is to give your rabbit a dose of Ivermectin (actually a horse de-wormer).
Fur Mites	When a rabbit has fur mites you should be able to tell due to the fact that it will begin losing fur in places such as the face, neck and back.	Just like Ear Mites, Fur Mites are caused by a mite that infests the rabbit.	The best way to get rid of fur mites is to rinse your rabbit off with some cat shampoo. Alternatively you can give your rabbit an oral dose of Ivermectin.
Warbles	Symptoms of Warbles include; swelling on or around the neck and the development of lumps slightly different from abscesses which contain a small "breathing hole".	Warbles are caused by a type of botfly that can infest your rabbitry.	In order to treat this parasitic condition you must enlarge the breathing hole of the parasite and carefully remove it from the enlarged hole. After removal you should apply an antiseptic ointment to the open wound.

| Internal Parasitic Conditions ||||
Negative Condition	Symptoms	Cause	Treatment
Pin Worms	When a rabbit acquires internal pin worms the symptoms are usually mild unless extreme infestation takes place. Rabbits that have pin worms will generally be harder to keep in good condition. Lack of fur condition can be an early indicator that a rabbit has pin worms.	Pin worms are caused by a particular parasite called Passalurus ambiguus.	It is recommended that you seek advice from a rabbit health specialist, to choose an appropriate de-wormer to give your rabbit. The best way to prevent your rabbits from getting worms in the first place is to try your best to improve the sanitation of your barn.
Tapeworms	Normally a rabbit that has tapeworms will act and look the same as a rabbit without them. Tapeworms do not usually produce visible signs on their host.	Tapeworms are transported to new hosts through larva. Generally you will only have tapeworm trouble in your rabbitry if you have dogs and cats hanging out nearby.	I wouldn't recommend getting too worried about tapeworms due to the fact that they are usually harmless. I suppose a de-wormer would get rid of them.

Non Infectious Conditions			
Negative Condition	Symptoms	Cause	Treatment
Fetal Giantism	Signs that your rabbit is going to have a fetal giant include; difficult birthing, late kindling and bleeding of the vulva. Fetal Giantism often leads to the death of either the doe or her kits.	Fetal Giantism usually takes place when a doe is excessively fat and only has 1 to 2 kits inside of her. The kits end up growing too large causing birthing complications, many times leading to death.	There isn't much you can do from a practical standpoint to help the doe, except to minimize stress and hope for the best. If the doe is extremely special or you have an emotional attachment to her you can always attempt to have a C-Section done. (for a high price of course)
Fur Ball	When a rabbit has a fur ball it often will exhibit symptoms including; diarrhea, loss of appetite, molting and loss of flesh condition.	A "Fur Ball" is primarily caused by the blockage of the stomach or intestine with fur which prevents ingested food from properly flowing down the intestinal track.	Give your rabbit a half tsp. of mineral oil for 3 days in a row. Perform this treatment for several weeks.
Slobbers	Your rabbit could have "Slobbers" if it begins to consistently salivate and develops an unusually wet dewlap or face.	The condition of "Slobbers" can be caused by multiple circumstances such as tooth problems or food contamination.	Remove the contaminated food from your rabbit's cage and try to give it some fresh dry grain. If something is wrong with a tooth try your best to have it treated or removed. (if the animal's well being is worth the additional expense to you)

Sore Hocks	Symptoms that your rabbit has sore hocks include; loss of hair on the hock region, scabby or sore looking development underneath the rabbit's foot, and possibly a noticeable decrease of condition or activeness.	Sore hocks can be caused by a lack of cage cleanliness or by a genetic problem. **Quick Tip**: Some breeders recommend placing a small wooden board in your rabbit's cage for it to rest its feet on to help prevent this condition.	Treat the sore hock with an astringent daily until the spot is healed up. In order to help prevent this condition try keeping your cages clean and make sure your breed stock have nice well padded hocks.
Wet Dewlap	A "Wet Dewlap" is a very obvious condition that a rabbit can acquire. If a rabbit has a wet dewlap you will notice that their dewlap is exceptionally moist looking and might even be green.	When a rabbit lays its chin in its water bowl for too long, particularly during the summer it can acquire a "Wet Dewlap". **Quick Prevention Tip**: Use rabbit water bottles instead of bowls.	If a rabbit develops a wet dewlap I simply recommend neatly cutting off its fur in that region. Some experts recommend applying antibiotic ointment to the location however from my experience the condition will eventually go away on its own.

Part 5: Marketing and Selling Your Rabbits

Selling Rabbits Overview

Over the years I have observed that the key factor which contributes to or takes away from the success of any rabbitry is the owner's ability to sell and market their rabbits. If you don't know how to market or sell your rabbits, your likelihood of success plummets. Even if you are only involved in the rabbit raising industry for a hobby you will still need to be able to get rid of excess stock. Not only will holding onto excess stock cost you time and money it will also negatively hinder your ability to achieve the goal of your rabbitry. I know this might sound like a shocking statement to make however I strongly suggest that you take my word on this matter. If you show rabbits you may have the best stock in the world, but if you fail to sell off excess stock you most likely will never be able to put winning show stock on the table.

The Rabbitry Examination

I recently decided to do an examination on a group of rabbitries, with marketing success being the differentiating criteria. The rabbitries greatly varied in size and ranged from commercial to hobby to home meat production rabbit farms. Here is a list of things that I observed based upon the given criteria...

Qualities of a Rabbitry with a "Marketing, Selling Problem"
- Breeding rabbits often have to be crowded into hutches due to herd overpopulation
- Many times herd overpopulation leads to another problem such as poor herd management
- Owners are constantly falling behind on management tasks
- Sometimes the owners get overwhelmed and decide to quit raising rabbits altogether
- Show animals tend to not perform as well as the owner would have hoped
- Herd illnesses may be more prevalent due to lack of disease control and cleanliness
- Out of disparity the owner may begin to increase their stock prices in order to help cover the cost of the additional feed they are buying

Qualities of a Rabbitry with a Successful Marketing Plan in Place
- Rabbitry generally is cleaner than most and well organized
- Breeding rabbits have cages of their own to reside in
- The owner does a better job at keeping accurate rabbitry records
- Rabbitry management chores are generally preformed in a more time efficient manner
- If they participate in showing the owners will often have good success with their rabbits on the judging table
- Most importantly the owners will have a fun and enjoyable rabbit raising experience

So hopefully from the rabbitry evaluation listed above you can begin to see the importance of developing a rabbitry marketing plan. The good news is I believe I can help you develop a successful rabbitry marketing plan in the next few pages of this book, "so don't get your feathers all flustered", as my mother used to say.

Rabbit Selling Outlets

First things first, before discussing marketing plans I want to evaluate some different rabbit selling outlets...

Rabbit Meat Market

The most popular outlet to sell excess rabbits to is the rabbit meat market. If people didn't consume rabbit meat there probably wouldn't even be half of the interest in rabbit raising that there is today. Even if you choose not to consume rabbit meat yourself you most likely will at least indirectly help supply this market with meat. If you breed rabbits you will most likely be doing one of the following three things; eating rabbit yourself, selling rabbits for meat or lastly selling breeding stock that produce meat for either another rabbit raiser or market. Of course if you plan on simply raising up a small pet rabbit breed you may be exempt from the rule.

There are actually three different ways that you can earn money off of rabbit meat:
- Sell Live Meat Rabbits
- Sell Rabbit Meat in Packages
- Sell Rabbits to your own Freezer

Live Meat Rabbits

The easiest way to cover rabbitry expenses is to sell live meat rabbits to either processors or local markets. I personally sell off most of my excess stock in this way through a contact that I have in the city of Houston, Texas. This way I don't have to deal with all the work involved with slaughtering and processing rabbits.

Sell Rabbit Meat

If you are desperate to get rid of rabbits the best option for you might be to slaughter and process the rabbits yourself and then sell the meat. I personally know quite a few people who would buy rabbit meat however they want no part in processing the rabbits themselves.

Sell Rabbits to your Freezer

If you don't have a problem with processing or eating your own rabbits, you will be able to sell rabbit directly to your freezer. Although you usually won't make any money off of this method, if you do things right you may just be able to save some money off your weekly grocery bill by eating home grown rabbit meat.

Breeding Stock Market

Most of the time the selling of rabbit breeding stock is what gives you the potential to make a good profit off of your rabbit expedition. Each year I keep around 20 percent of my best quality rabbits that I have born to raise up for the breeding stock market. The majority of my other rabbits are sold to the meat market for about a breakeven price. If my main focus wasn't on raising up show rabbits, I would probably sell a larger percentage of my herd animals as breeding stock to increase profits. The key to earning money off of breeding stock animals is to focus on quality not quantity. Keep this statement in mind: Most buyers want to purchase the best animals that their money can buy, not just as many as they can buy.

Laboratory Market

Once you have become an established rabbit breeder with a good reputation and large herd you might just be able to sell some of your excess stock to the laboratory market. One of the main purposes of the rabbit laboratory market is to test out skin products that are made for humans. Supposedly rabbits and humans have similarities in their skin reactions. I also have heard that some pharmaceutical and medical companies still perform "experiments" on rabbits to test out new products. Although the laboratory market turns many rabbit raisers off due to the fact that they worry about the fate of their beloved rabbits, nowadays there are pretty strict regulations in place for animal experimentation.

Pet Market

Over the last two decades the rabbit pet market has grown tremendously. If you are breeder who breeds a small to medium size rabbit breed you may just be in a great position to take advantage of this growing trend! I personally do not sell very many rabbits to the pet market due to the fact that I am currently raising Californian meat rabbits. I personally wouldn't recommend very many of the larger breeds for pet purposes. Besides I have been in the habit of keeping rabbits based upon meat qualities instead of tameness for years now. So in general many of my rabbits aren't exactly the tamest of chaps.

Deciding on a Fair Price

Before putting your rabbits up for sale it is important to decide upon a fair price. When I price my rabbits I try to come up with an honest price primarily based upon the cost of feed and the value of my time. As like any other business or hobby at first you may be forced to work without much monetary compensation. I know quite a few dedicated rabbit raisers who have never made much money off of their rabbits however they continue to enjoy their rabbit experience. The important thing is that you enjoy your new hobby and or business. Also I advise you to take into consideration the value of the knowledge that you have learned from your rabbit project. If you knew my personal story you would realize that even if I never had made a penny off of my rabbits the learning experience would have definitely still made the endeavor worthwhile. If you take time to think about it, I bet you will be surprised how much you can learn from just raising rabbits! Whatever you do, never underestimate the value of hands on learning.

So now that I have got that philosophy off my chest, let us continue… I personally price my breeding stock at approximately $60-100 each, my pet rabbits at around $50 and my meat rabbits at an average market price. I believe this is a pretty fair price system considering the quality of my animals. Over the years, I have had several breeders come up to me and tell me that I am "leaving money on the table". Yes that may be so; however one of the main purposes behind continuing my rabbit project is to help other rabbit raisers get started. *Now let me ask you a question*; how considerate would it be of me to charge several hundred dollars per average breeding stock animal when one of my main markets is selling to 4-H and FFA students?

Quick Tip: I recommend that you price your average breeding stock somewhere between $40-100 each. If you raise a rare or giant breed or simply have a really excellent animal for sale, you can charge more than this. I just recommend that you keep your average prices in this range for breeding stock. Pet rabbits can usually be sold for around $30-100 each (depending upon breed and rarity) and meat rabbits generally need to be sold at an average market price or nobody will buy them. Generally meat buyers will pay between $1-1.75 per pound of live rabbit.

Like always you are free to do what you wish with your rabbit project… you can charge whatever prices you wish and can sell as many animals as the market will buy. I however advise you to consider my advice on setting prices; not only will this help you sell more rabbits it will also help you acquire a good reputation. If you do things right you can still make a decent profit without overcharging your market. ☺

Online Rabbit Advertising

Several years ago it was much harder to market your rabbits than it is today. With the boom of the internet, rabbitry advertising has become a lot easier. In this article we will be examining some of the most popular ways to market your rabbitry on the internet.

Online Classifieds

The best to promote your rabbitry online in the year 2015 and beyond is to use a service I helped get started available via SellRabbitsOnDemand.com. Essentially by becoming a member of this low cost "Sell Rabbits on Demand" service, you will acquire the ability to post virtually unlimited unique rabbit classifieds on our high traffic + targeted rabbit website network. At the time of writing this article our main website (RabbitBreeders.us) has received approximately 5 million visits. So as you can probably already imagine… this service has the potential to be extremely useful to your rabbitry.

Check it out: http://SellRabbitsOnDemand.com/

Listing your Rabbitry in Breeders Directories

Another great way for the average rabbit raiser to market their rabbitry online in 2015 and beyond (in addition to using the SellRabbitsOnDemand.com system) is to submit to rabbit breeders' directories. A year ago this technique wouldn't have been nearly as effective as it is now. Since the establishment of my USA Rabbit Breeders directory in January of 2011, everything has begun to change. Before setting up the site I noticed that almost all of the rabbit breeders directories on the web were either outdated or simply too small to make a significant difference. I had the vision of creating a huge rabbit breeders directory network which would eventually cover every country, state and province in the world. I know this sounds a bit crazy but I believe my vision shall come true someday.

The directory network that I established already encompasses three major countries; the United States, Canada and England. If I can find somebody to help me translate basic website content to other languages I can expand this directory network to eventually include Non English speaking countries too! I know I already get frequent English speaking visitors from places around the World like India, South Africa, Egypt and the Philippines.

Submit your Rabbitry to the Leading Directory Network

To help make sure that you are able to take advantage of this free directory advertising opportunity I have written up a step by step tutorial which should guide you through the submission process...

Step 1: Visit your country's breeder's directory...
- United States: http://rabbitbreeders.us/
- Canada: http://www.rabbitbreeders.ca/
- England: http://rabbitbreeders.org.uk/

Step 2: Take a few minutes to browse around the website. Be sure to check out the state-province rabbit breeders' index and the breed index to get an idea of what your rabbitry submission will look like.

Step 3: Visit the Submit a Rabbitry tab on the site navigation bar. Fill out the form on the page by filling in your first name and email address.

Step 4: Within a few minutes you will receive a confirmation email. Inside the email there is a confirmation link which you must click on to verify your newsletter subscription in order to get your rabbitry listed in our directory. We will never share your email address with any other

company without your written permission. You also have the option to unsubscribe from our newsletter at any time.

Step 5: After you confirm your subscription to our newsletter you will receive an automated email from our system which provides you with a special directory submission link.

Step 6: Once you receive the email click the link that takes you to the submission page. You should now see a form similar to the one shown below:

Free Rabbitry Submission

Like 5 people like this

Thanks for subscribing to the rabbit breeders newsletter! Now you can add your rabbitry to our rabbit breeders list using the simple form below ☺ .

When submitting please remember that the more information you provide about your rabbitry the more likely you will be noticed by buyers! (Hint provide a good amount of information in the rabbitry description box: Who you are, Why you raise rabbits, Info about your herd, estimate rabbit herd size, What types of rabbits you raise, Member of ARBA? - if so provide registration number, In 4-H or FFA?, etc..)

Your Name (Example: Joey Carter) (required)

Your Email (Example: joeycarter@gmail.com) (required)

Your City, State (Example: Woodlands, Texas) (required)

Your Postal Address + Zip Code (Example: 12345 Cedar Land Dr. 82313) (recommended)

Your Phone Number (Example: 670-998-1022) (recommended)

Rabbitry Name (Example: Golden B Rabbitry) (required)

Step 7: I recommend that you take at least 10 to 15 minutes to accurately fill out the form. It is required that you provide your; Name, Email, City, State or Province, Rabbit Breeds, Main Rabbit Breed, Rabbitry Name and lastly a rabbitry description. The website, phone number and postal address fields are completely optional.

Please Note: As always your information will stay safe with us. We will not sell or give your information to anyone without your written permission.

Note: You can control what part of your contact information is shown on the rabbitry listing pages by using the checkboxes at the bottom of the form. For instance you are required to provide us with your email address so that we can contact you if need be. If you don't want your email address listed on the directory pages don't check the box next to email.

What is the best way for buyers to contact you? (required)
☐ By Phone ☐ By Email ☐ By Mail ☐ My Website

[Send]

Rabbit Breeds: There are two different rabbit breed fields that you are required to fill out. One is titled Rabbit Breeds and the other is titled Main Rabbit Breed. Please list all of your rabbit breeds including your main breed in the Rabbit Breeds form field. Next select **ONE** rabbit breed to be chosen as your "main rabbit breed". Even if you have two "main breeds" **please only type one into this box**.

Rabbit Breeds (Example: New Zealands, Mini Rex) (required)
Californian, New Zealand

Main Rabbit Breed (Select only one here) (Example: Californians) (required)
Californian

I will post your rabbitry on your specific state- province directory page. I will also list your contact information on **ONE rabbit breed directory page**. (On the directory page of the breed that you selected as your "main" breed)

State Page Listing: Below I have provided an example image of what your state or province page listing will look like... (Email address of owner has been blotted out in order to help maintain their privacy)

State Listing Example

Lea Kirby
Woodland, CA
Mini Lop, Mini Rex, Polish, Californians
Thumper's Friends Rabbitry
My four daughters and I have a small scale rabbitry. We currently breed Mini Lops, Mini Rex, Polish and Californians. We do have rabbits for sale frequently and post them on our for sale page. My daughters are involved in 4-H and FFA. We attend as many shows as we can and post our results and pictures on our website. We are open to co-operative breeding and information sharing. We are located in Woodland, California, approximately 30 miles from Sacramento in Northern California.

Breed Page Listing: Below is a picture of the same rabbitry's breed listing, (contact info has been blotted out to help maintain privacy). **Notice that the rabbitry description does not show up on this page**. (There is actually a good reason for this; maybe I will share it with you another time)

Breed Listing Example

Lea Kirby
Woodland, California
Thumper's Friends Rabbitry
www.thumpersfriendsrabbitry.com

Indiana

Rabbitry Description: Be sure to write up an in-depth paragraph description of your rabbitry. See above for an example of what you can put in this field.

Quick Tip: Having a nice description here will help distinguish your rabbitry from the rest of the listings.

Website URL: After you fill out the rabbitry description field if you have a website you can put the URL into the website form field. If you have a website of your own please take the time to add a simple clickable text link to our directory somewhere on your website. Also by linking to our site you will have an opportunity to get your rabbitry featured on our rabbit breeders' directory! I will discuss featured rabbitries in a minute. ☺

Step 8: Once you have filled out the form fields, be sure to read over your listing information. You wouldn't believe how many forms with typos I receive on a weekly basis! Then HIT SUBMIT!

Step 9: Submit the form, and check your email inbox again for an automated confirmation email. The email will contain information about how you can update your listing information at a later date if need be. I will post your listing as soon as I get the chance! ☺ GOOD LUCK!

How to get your Rabbitry Featured Online

If you are lucky enough you might be able to get your rabbitry featured on one of the popular rabbit websites on the internet. At Rabbit Empire we choose rabbitries to be featured based upon certain criteria on a frequent basis. Here are some tips and tricks for getting your rabbitry featured online...

1. Submit your rabbitry to our directory network (see the previous few pages for step by step instructions)
2. Be sure to fill out the form fields to the best of your ability and provide an in-depth rabbitry description.
3. Do NOT write the exact same rabbitry description for multiple online rabbitry directories. Be unique, express yourself!
4. If you have a website of your own, be sure to write up good content and supply pictures of your rabbitry on the site.
5. If you list your rabbitry url on the directory listing be sure to add a link to the directory site somewhere on your site to help return the favor. Be sure to make the link clickable so that directory owners will be notified after you post the link to their site.
6. If the directory has any type of forum or blog be sure to actively leave comments. This will help you get noticed by the directory owner.
7. Become a fan of their facebook page if they have one. At rabbitbreeders.us we have a popular rabbit breeder's fan page that you are free to advertise your rabbitry on! Check it out: http://facebook.com/USARabbitBreeders

In addition to getting free rabbitry exposure there are other benefits to getting your rabbitry featured. From time to time we may give away special prizes to the owners of featured rabbitries!

Good Luck on Getting your Rabbitry Featured :)

Local Rabbitry Advertising

If you follow my advice on local rabbitry advertising you will hopefully be able to find enough customers who are willing to buy rabbits from you...

Business Cards

I highly recommend that you never underestimate the effectiveness of rabbitry business cards. Recently I found out that one of the major rabbitries in my area runs there marketing campaign almost solely off of business cards. I recommend that you use a program such as Microsoft Publisher or OpenOffice to create business cards for your rabbitry.

Quick Tip: I recommend giving each of your customers three of your rabbitry business cards. If your customers are happy with their rabbits it is a good bet that they will end up passing out these cards to their friends. After making a rabbitry sale hand the cards to your customer and ask them something like; "If you know of anyone else who is looking for rabbits, feel free to send them our way."

Flyer Promotion

Flyers are another great way to find customers locally. Type up some rabbitry flyers in a program such as Microsoft Publisher and begin hanging these flyers up on local bulletin boards. You might just be surprised how many people still glance at these boards! The best place to distribute flyers is at your local feed store and county extension office. Many people will check these places when they are in search of livestock or pets.

Quick Tip: It is a good idea to try your best to become friends with your county extension office staff. These people usually can help you locate buyers in your area and recommend potential customers to your rabbitry. Be sure to give these people at least one of your flyers or business cards.

Ask Around Town

If you have lived in the same town for quite awhile you are bound to know people who would be willing to buy rabbits for either meat or pets. If you process your rabbits yourself, there most likely will be plenty of locals who will be willing to order rabbit meat from you. Just ask around, and tell your friends to ask their friends. After awhile of doing this type of promotion you are bound to run into either potential customers or friends who know potential customers!

Contact Management

It is important to make sure that potential buyers have a good way to contact you. If you distribute local promotional material I recommend that you either place your phone number or email address on the material. If you have a website URL, be sure to put that on the promotional material too however make certain that buyers have an alternate way to contact you other than through the internet.

Phone Number

It is a good idea to distribute your home phone number instead of your cell number on promotional material. Ideally if you have a fulltime rabbit business you will have your own business phone number however if you don't just include your home phone number. It can get rather annoying to have buyers calling you up on your mobile phone when you are trying to get work done. I ask customers to leave a message on my home phone answering machine and then answer calls once every few days.

Email Address

Email is a good way to communicate with potential customers online. In fact most breeder directories including rabbitbreeders.us list the email addresses of rabbit breeders on the listing pages. I recommend that you make a special email address for your rabbitry. You can go to gmail.com and create a free email account. If you ever change email addresses, instead of trying to update your breeder listings and promotional material I recommend just forwarding the messages to your new email address.

Website

I use my rabbitry website to reach out to potential customers in my state. A website is a great way to reach potential customers however it is not the only way. Many successful rabbitries that I know of don't have rabbitry websites setup and still have customers lined up throughout the entire year. A great alternate to a website is a service called SellRabbitsOnDemand.com that allows you to post unlimited unique rabbit classifieds on RabbitBreeders.us and other websites.

Developing a Good Reputation

When you are running any type of business it is important to develop a good reputation amongst customers and potential buyers. Here are some tips which will help you develop a good rabbitry reputation...

1. Offer reasonable prices
2. Be sure to help your customers get started with their rabbit adventure
3. Answer questions that your customers send you to the best of your ability
4. Give your customers a honest evaluation of the rabbits that you are selling them
5. Show kindness to others
6. Attend any local rabbit meetings or clinics that are put on in your area
7. If you make a mistake be sure to apologize
8. Lastly, be yourself and have a good time! :)

Additional Rabbit Revenue Streams

It is always nice to be able to make additional revenue off of your rabbit project even if you are only into rabbit raising for a hobby. In my opinion there are two main ways that you can begin to earn extra income off of your rabbit project...

1. Fertilizer
2. Worms

Fertilizer: Yes I said it; you can actually make extra money off of your rabbit project by selling rabbit manure as plant fertilizer! Rabbit manure is by far one of the most valuable types of fertilizer on the planet! Rabbit food is high in protein and quality which results in the natural development of a very high quality rabbit manure. Back when I was in Middle School I did a comprehensive science fair project (which earned a blue first place ribbon- by the way) on the effects of different types of fertilizers on plant growth. I experimented using several different types of manure and store bought commercial fertilizers on forty different pots of grass. In the long term experiment it turned out that rabbit manure outperformed the professional store bought fertilizer! So yes rabbit fertilizer is indeed valuable to people who plant gardens and it even works great if you apply it to orchards.

Worms: In addition to selling fertilizer you can also grow your own worms under your rabbit hutches to sell for fish bait or experimental purposes.

How to Make Money Selling Fertilizer

Here is a step by step guide to making extra rabbit money by selling your rabbitry's waste products as fertilizer...

Step 1: Find a Good Location to Build a Compost Pile: I recommend finding a partially shaded area to start building up your rabbit compost pit. Try picking an area that is fairly close to your rabbit hutches so that you won't have to haul rabbit manure too far.

Step 2: Start Building the Pile: There are several different ways that you can build a compost pile however I prefer to use the "piling method". After finding a good location for the compost pit I suggest that you map out the dimensions of the pile in your mind. Next lay down a layer of organic materials such as leaves or cut grass on the ground. After you lay down a layer of organic materials I suggest that you go to your rabbit hutches with a wheel barrow and shovel and bring back your first load of rabbit manure. Now dump the rabbit manure on top of the layer of organic material and go back to get a few more loads. Once you have built up a decent sized pile of rabbit manure on top of the organic material I suggest that you add one more layer on top of the pile. This top layer should simply consist of soil. Some people have recommended repeating this 3 layer process again on top of the pile that you just created. For beginners I just recommend sticking with the 3 layer method.

Step 3: Leave to Decompose: I suggest that you leave the pile that you created untouched for several months to give it time to decompose. In the mean time you can begin starting more piles to build up additional revenue sources.

Step 4: Harvest Time: Once your rabbit manure pile has decomposed you should have a rich soil filled without valuable nutrients. If the pile is dry enough I will simply use old 50 pound rabbit grain bags to bag up the stuff to sell. (This way I don't have to spend any money on packaging material and can reuse the grain bags)

Step 5: Sell the Stuff: Now it is time to begin making some extra money selling garden fertilizer! There is a good chance that you know at least a few gardeners already that would love to have your composted rabbit manure for fertilizer. Simply give them a holler and see if they would like any homemade fertilizer for their garden. Alternatively you can take a picture of the fertilizer and sell it on sites like Craigslist. A good way to get first time customers is to give away free samples or offer your fertilizer for a low price. I have seen some people bag up manure in 50 pound grain bags and sell it for $10/bag (sometimes this is only slightly lower than they buy the actual grain for!). Talk about making some nice extra spending money! :)

Make Money Growing and Selling Worms

Here is a step by step guide which covers the basics on how to start making money by growing and selling worms...

Step 1: Plan out your Worm Project: The first thing you need to do is decide on how many worms you want to buy and where you plan on growing them. It has been recommended by many worm experts to start out with at least 2,500 worms. Although this number seems quite large many people recommend planting at least 1,000 worms for every doe and litter you have! It is also recommended that you keep your worms directly under hanging rabbit cages in "worm beds". This way the worms will have a constant supply of food and they will help you out by eliminating the odor in your rabbit barns.

Step 2: Build the Worm Beds: Your worm beds can be built using rectangular 1" x 12" boards. The boards can be nailed together to form a rectangular worm bed under your rabbit cages. Some people choose to use 1" x 8" boards instead however others claim that the 1" x 12" boards help your worms by giving them a deeper "bed" to reside in.

Step 3: Apply Bedding: It is recommended that you place some type of worm bedding inside of your worm beds. Some worm growers recommend using old sawdust or peat moss for worm bedding.

Step 4: Purchase the worms: There are different places that you can order worms from. I suggest that you do a search online to try and locate worm breeders.

Step 5: Let them Grow: If possible it is best to keep your rabbits in a warm environment so they don't freeze. If everything goes well your worms should begin to multiple fast!

Step 6: Harvest your Worms: It is recommended that you clean out your worm beds at least twice a year and sell a large number of your worms. The biggest market for worms is the ever growing fishing industry! If you live in an area where lots of people fish like I do, selling your worms shouldn't be too hard. Just offer good deals at competitive prices and I am sure you will be able to sell some worms to at least your fishing friends. Although I haven't tried this yet, I bet you can land some worm sales by simply posting ads on sites like Craigslist. You can also sell the soil in the worm beds as potting soil to gardeners for additional income.

Good Luck and Happy Worm Growing!

Part 6: Interesting Resources + Additional Articles

Raising Rabbits in the Sizzling Summer

If you live in a hot southern climate like me you will be faced with the daunting task of taking care of your rabbits in the sizzling summer heat. As I write this article from my home in Texas, we have been experiencing the hottest summer weather since the year 1906 (according to a report by Fox News)! It can get a bit annoying having to go out in 100 degrees + heat on a daily basis to take care of all your rabbits however it is definitely much more challenging on the rabbits than it is on us. Imagine yourself stuck in a fur coat living outside 24 hours a day when the night time temperature stays above 90 degrees… unfortunately that is the situation that most rabbits living in the southern US are facing this year. So in this article I have provided some tips, tricks and solutions that you can deploy to help your rabbits make it through the heat…

What can happen when a rabbit overheats?

- Bucks can go sterile for several months if they are kept in a too hot of environment
- Rabbits can lose condition and eat less food
- Many times your bucks will go into molts and temporarily lose most of their hair
- Lastly when a rabbit gets too overheated they can die from heat stroke

So as you can see too much heat can be a big and potentially dangerous problem for rabbits. I personally have had quite a few rabbits die over the years due to the summer heat. However, I have been much more fortunate than many other rabbit raisers that I know which have lost some of their best breeding stock over the summer months.

The Ideal Cooling Solution

Although the majority of rabbit raisers don't possess this luxury, the ideal cooling solution for your rabbitry is an Air Conditioned Barn. Outside hutches work great during the fall, winter and spring however during the summer they can flat out get too hot. The drawback of air conditioned buildings is the expense. Also if you live in a subdivision, there is a good chance that you won't be allowed to simply install an air conditioned barn in your backyard. Note: Only a couple rabbit raisers that I know possess their own air conditioned rabbit barns.

Cooling Tips for the Rest of Us

So most likely an air conditioned barn is out of the question, at least for the majority of us rabbit raisers. Here is a list of tips and tricks that I recommend using to keep your rabbits cool…

- The number one way to help keep your rabbits cool without an AC unit is to keep them in the shade during the day. Ideally you would use trees to shade your rabbit building or hutches however if you don't have trees over your hutches you can try to setup a tent-like enclosure to shield your rabbits from the suns direct rays.
- Setup fans or evaporative coolers inside your rabbit building. If you setup fans be sure that you hook them up in a well ventilated area or you might risk making the situation worse by blowing hot air on your rabbits.
- If you only have a few rabbits I recommend freezing two litter coke bottles and placing them in your rabbit cages twice a day. If you don't have enough time available to use this method, simply try placing frozen bottles in your bucks' cages. Bucks will tend to suffer the worst during heat spells.
- If you have beloved pet rabbits, maybe try moving them indoors for the summer.
- Turn on sprinklers next to your rabbit building. Believe it or not this method works great to lower the temperature of the area. When the water that gets sprayed in the air evaporates it naturally cools down.
- Avoid keeping multiple rabbits in the same cage. When you have multiple rabbits sharing a cage, their shared body heat contributes to a hotter living environment.
- Make ventilation holes in your rabbit building. When I first began raising rabbits my dad and I literally cut a hole in the side of a totally enclosed storage building to allow for better ventilation for the rabbits.

Breeding Rabbits in the summer

If you live in an environment where the average summer temperature is above 85 degrees, if possible I recommend not breeding at all during the summer months. From personal experience I have noticed that bunnies tend to have the hardest time dealing with the heat. In fact this year I have lost quite a few bunnies during this heat wave that has encompassed my state.

If you need to breed your rabbits for a show in the summer months I recommend that you use all wire nest boxes to help keep your newborn kits cool. Alternatively you can take your nest boxes indoors for the day and bring them back outside in the evening. If neither option works for you, simply be sure to keep your rabbits in a well shaded environment and maybe try running a sprinkler.

Regardless of what you decide... Good Luck and Keep Them Rabbits Cool!!!

Raising Rabbits in the Winter

For me and other southern rabbit breeders the winter time is usually a wonderful time to be raising rabbits. The weather is usually nice and cool but not too cold. With 40 degree nights and 60 degree days our rabbits stay healthy and happy in their hutches. The long summer is over and all the rabbits seem to be more active, excitingly hopping around their cages. Far off from our world rabbit raisers in the colder climates prepare for their most difficult season of the year. In this article I will be sharing with you a few tips and tricks to help keep your rabbits warm in the winter…

The Good News

As you worry about the health of your rabbits during the long and cold winter, I want to give you some good news for a change. Rabbits are naturally suited for doing well in cold climates! Remember rabbits have a nice, warm and fuzzy fur coat that thickens in the winter. Northern rabbit raisers have informed me that adult rabbits can fairly easily tolerate temperatures as low as 0 degrees Fahrenheit.

Keeping your Rabbits Warm

The ideal solution for keeping rabbits warm during the winter is to have a heated barn that at least keeps the temperature above freezing at all times. The downfall to heated barns will of course be the additional utility expense. If you can't afford to setup a heated barn there are still things that you can do to help keep your rabbits warm…

- Move any outside rabbits into an enclosed building if possible. Buildings will at least help keep the rabbits protected from cold wind gusts.
- Cover any openings in your rabbit building with tarp, wood or plastic during extremely cold weather. I personally will hang up sheets of plastic on the sides of my open rabbit buildings during the winter.
- Try covering up your rabbit cages during the night with old sheets or towels.
- Hang up heat lamps in your rabbit building.
- Place some hay inside of your rabbit cages for your rabbits to lie on.

The Water Solution

One important thing that you must do if you live in a climate that constantly freezes over is to make sure that your rabbits' water supply doesn't freeze too. Some breeders have moved to using heated rabbit water bottles in the winter to solve this problem. You actually can buy heated rabbit water bottles at a store such as Amazon for a quite reasonable price. If you have an automatic rabbit watering system it is a good idea to wrap it up in heat tape to help prevent the pipe from freezing. During freezes I will let my automatic rabbit watering system drip from the end to prevent the whole pipe from freezing.

Some breeders including myself recommend that you keep rabbit bowls on hand just in case something happens to your main watering system during the winter months.

Whatever you decide to do to protect your rabbit water supply do remember that if your rabbits go without water for too long the consequences can be detrimental.

Breeding Rabbits in the Winter

As long as you don't live in a super cold environment it is still ok to breed your rabbits during the winter months. (If you do live in a super cold environment, don't worry because you will still be able to breed your rabbits during the spring, summer and fall.)

The most important thing that you can do to get your rabbits to breed in the winter is to make sure that they get an appropriate amount of light each day. Rabbits naturally will be more apt to breed when they have more hours of daylight. In the wild this instinct trait helps encourage rabbits to reproduce when the weather is right. You can artificially give your rabbits "daylight" by hanging up lights in your rabbit building or next to your rabbit hutches. I recommend that you try to give your rabbits at least twelve hours of light during breeding season. I personally will rig up a light in my rabbit barns several weeks before breeding and leave it on from between 5 p.m. and 8 p.m. to help give my rabbits more "daylight". If you wish you can buy lights with timer settings at the store, to help make your life easier. Some rabbit breeders will even keep lights on their rabbits all day from around 6 a.m. to 9 p.m. Just do what works best for you and your rabbits!

Lastly with regard to the process of kindling and giving birth I want to make a recommendation…

In the winter I recommend that you give your does' wooden nest boxes filled with hay to help keep your new born kits warm. For more info on birthing rabbits check out our kindling section in part 2 of this book.

Good Luck and Stay Warm!!

Showing Rabbits

How to Show Rabbits. In this article I will be introducing you to the exciting topic of showing rabbits for 4-H, FFA and or ARBA breed shows.

What is a rabbit show?

Many people are surprised to find that there's a thriving hobby in this country called showing rabbits. Really, they ask, do people show rabbits like horses or dogs? The answer is yes! That is, it's somewhat like horses or dogs.

Rabbit shows are unique in that the animals don't compete against each other so much as the breeders do. In horse or dog shows, each animal is very important; you can be a successful showman even if you have only one horse or dog. In rabbit shows, breeders bring their current "show string" of bunnies to compare them to their competition, then take them back home and put them in the breeding pen to produce the next generation of winners.

Rabbit shows are not based on performance; they are judged almost entirely on the animal's physical appearance. Judges compare the bunnies to each other and to the written ideal of each breed in the Standard of Perfection published by the American Rabbit Breeders Association (ARBA). Classes are divided by breed, color, sex, and age. The smaller rabbit breeds have two age classifications: junior (under six months) and senior (over six months). The larger breeds also have an intermediate division, (between six and eight months) and the senior class is over eight months.

What does a good show rabbit look like?

Not every rabbit can be entered in a show. All show rabbits must be purebred, and not every purebred rabbit will be of a quality to do well. There is vast variety in show rabbits — some are long-limbed and hare-like, others are short and round, some have lopped ears, others have stubby upright ones, some have woolly coats, some have plush coats – but there are a few traits that they all share. All show rabbits must have excellent fur and flesh condition; their bodies must be smooth and solid. They must be balanced in body, head, and ear shape and length. Every breed has its own ideal qualities, and it can take some time to learn exactly what to look for as you select your production animals. All rabbits entered in a show must have a permanent number tattooed in their left ear.

The best place to learn what to look for in a show bunny is a rabbit show itself. There you can watch judges evaluate hundreds of animals and give remarks about each one. There you can talk to breeders, many of whom are happy to show you their animals and teach you how to apply the Standard. And the showroom is even a good place to buy a few bunnies to start your own adventure.

How do you enter a rabbit show?

Shows are hosted by local clubs that are affiliated with 4-H or the American Rabbit Breeders Association. ARBA shows are divided into two categories: open and youth. Anyone may show in the "open" category, but only those between the ages of 5 and 19 can enter in "youth." No single rabbit can be shown in both open and youth on the same day. Usually only youth members are allowed to enter 4-H events.

To find a rabbit show in your area, visit the ARBA website or get in touch with your local 4-H leader or extension office. Then contact the show secretary and ask for a flyer or catalog. This document will give you the details on how and when to enter. Some shows are pre-entry, meaning that you need to mail or email in your entry before a certain deadline. Others are day-of-show entry. All shows accept entries in the same format: they need to know your name and address, and a few facts about each rabbit you enter, namely the breed, color, sex, age classification, and tattoo number. The only other thing you will need to provide is a small entry fee, usually about $3-4 per animal. Happy showing!

Learn more about Showing Rabbits (Two Recommended Books):

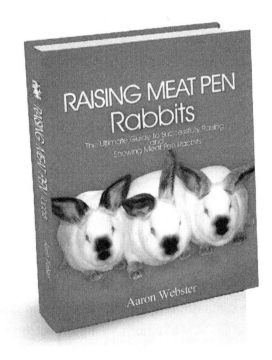

The Youth Rabbit Project Study Guide:
http://www.premiumrabbits.com/youth-rabbit-project-study-guide/

Raising Meat Pen Rabbits:
http://www.premiumrabbits.com/raising-meat-pen-rabbits/

Via Amazon: http://rabbitbreeders.us/AmazonMeatPenRabbits

Rabbit Color Genetics

Rabbit Color Genetics. Find information about rabbit coat color genetics and recommended resources on the subject in this article.

As daunting as it may sound to learn the genetics of every rabbit color, it's not actually very difficult to master the basics. We can break all rabbit colors into a few groups that greatly simplify a lesson on rabbit coat color genetics. For instance, have you ever noticed that there are only four basic rabbit colors? Black, blue, chocolate, and lilac.

Take any familiar variety, let's say Himalayan. A Himalayan colored rabbit is white with red eyes, and a touch of dark color on the nose, ears, feet and tail. (The color is also known as Californian or Pointed White, depending on the breed.) All "Himies" are white with red eyes – but what color are the markings? In most, they are a dark gray, essentially black. But not in all. Himalayans are also found with blue, chocolate, and lilac markings instead of black. Some breeds allow these other versions to be shown, some don't, but genetically they can exist in any breed.

All other rabbit colors are the same way. There are black otters, blue otters, chocolate otters, and lilac otters. Tortoise ("tort") can come with black, blue, chocolate, or lilac shading. Those are the obvious ones.

Photo below: black tort vs. blue tort

The color Chestnut is a black-based variety. If you look at the guard hairs, they are black. The ear lacing is black. The undercolor, the color of the hair shaft next to the skin, is slate gray. But chestnut comes in a blue-based version, too. We call it opal.

Opal is genetically the same color as chestnut, except that it is blue-based instead of black-based. In other words, it's the "diluted" form of chestnut. Where there hairs are black on chestnut, they are blue on an opal, and the orange color in chestnut is also diluted to a fawn color in opal.

There's a lilac-based version of chestnut, also. The common name for it in the US is lynx. The chocolate-based version of chestnut has different names in different breeds, but it looks just like a regular chestnut except that the black hairs are chestnut instead. This color is usually known as chocolate chestnut or chocolate agouti, but the Rex breed calls it "amber" and British standards call it "cinnamon."

Pretty cool, isn't it? For another example, the familiar color Siamese Sable is black-based. If you look at the shading where it's darkest, like on the nose, it's nearly black. We call the blue version Smoke Pearl. There genetically can be chocolate and lilac versions, too, but they don't look very different from sable and smoke, respectively. Thus, the chocolate and lilac versions don't really have their own names and aren't usually show-able. You'll find this with a lot of colors. The black and blue versions look quite a bit different and are recognized. Chocolate versions tend to look like faded black ones, and lilac versions look like poor blue ones. They aren't different enough to be counted as their own varieties, so usually don't get their own names.

For an educational challenge, try identifying the base color on the bunnies you see at the next show. Places to look for base color include guard hairs and ear lacing, and any dark shading. Also, eyes will be brown on black and chocolate-based colors, and blue-gray on the dilute varieties: blue and lilac.

When we realize that all rabbit varieties come in one of four basic colors, it drastically cuts down the number of genetic combinations that we need to learn! Instead of having to regard chestnut, opal, chocolate agouti, and lynx as four separate colors, we can count them as just one, in four different versions.

Photo below: Chestnut (called Castor in Mini Rex) vs. Opal

But how do the four basic colors relate to each other? Well, that's another lesson, but thankfully an easy one. In brief, black can be considered "normal." Blue is a dilute of black; blue has the same pigments as black, but the pigment granules are scattered in the hair shaft, allowing more light to pass through and "diluting" the appearance of the color.

Chocolate is something different altogether. Chocolate is not a dilute color. Chocolate is actually changing the color of the pigments from black to brown. And what is lilac? Here's where it gets fun: biochemically, lilac is both dilute and chocolate together. Lilac is a diluted chocolate, or in other words, a blue in which the normal pigment color has been changed to brown.

Curious to learn further? Color genetics becomes more and more fascinating the deeper you study it. If you're interested in discovering more about this important topic, and how to practically apply it to your advantage in your breeding program, check out "A Book About Bunny Colors," the practical breeder's guide to rabbit coat color. Written in easy language, this book places emphasis on the "what happens" with coat color genetics, not all the scientific why's and how's. It uses lots of charts and photos to help you grasp the information, and spells out how to apply it in your breeding. Check out the list of features below, and then grab your copy to unlock the mysteries of rabbit coat color!

65 pages. Printed in full color.

Table of Contents:

Chapter 1: Explaining how genes are passed on to offspring

Chapter 2: De-coding the genotypes of familiar rabbit colors

Chapter 3: Practical use of coat color genetics in your rabbit breeding

Chapter 4: Tips on improving your specific color breeding program

Chapter 5: The secondary coat color groups

Coat color glossary

Appendix A: Descriptions and genotypes of 50 familiar rabbit colors

Appendix B: Alternate names of rabbit varieties by breed

Appendix C: Sources for more information

Grab a Copy: http://www.premiumrabbits.com/the-rabbit-coat-colors-genetics-guide/

Managing Rabbits

Managing Rabbits. Information and resources on how to manage rabbits.

The old phrase "breed like rabbits" makes it sound like rabbit keeping is simple and easy. Just put the bunnies together and soon you have babies to sell, right? But we all know that there's more to it than that. Proper rabbit herd management requires a good deal of planning, the right rabbit supplies, and plenty of plain old hard work. Sure, it takes some significant effort, but the rewards are high.

A Successful Startup

No matter whether you're raising rabbits for pets, shows, meat, or another purpose, you'll need about the same equipment. Secure and sanitary are the keys when selecting proper rabbit housing. Most breeders opt for all-wire cages over wooden ones, as they are easier to clean and harder for the rabbit to escape from. Rabbits have sensitive respiratory tracts; they must be kept in a building with excellent airflow. The rabbitry should be quiet and kept free of predators and weather extremes if you want to give your rabbits the best chance of survival.

Of course, it's crucial to start with excellent breeding stock. The traits you look for in your start-up animals will vary based on your purpose for them, but never ever settle for rabbits that aren't in excellent health.

The Importance of Planning

You know that quote from Carlyle: "A man without a goal is like a ship without a rudder." Rabbitries work the same way. Managing rabbits successfully includes knowing what you are doing and why. Set a tangible goal for your herd and it will guide your husbandry practices, your breeding choices, and your record keeping. Don't just say, "I want to raise better show rabbits." Say instead, "I need to improve shoulders in my current show herd," or "I need to produce rabbits with better coat quality." Selection is everything when it comes to your breeding program. You can see improvement quickly when you pick a specific trait to improve and only keep replacements that are strong in that area. When you focus your efforts on one small project, you meet your goal quickly, and have the confidence to tackle the next step.

Managing Rabbits: Rely on a Schedule

Rabbits (and people too) always do better on schedules. Set a regular chore schedule and stick to it. If you just say, "I have to remember to clean cages soon," the job can get shoved aside for weeks. You should have a set time that you feed every day, and a set day to perform certain chores. For example, you could always empty trays on Saturdays, give your herd a health check on Sundays, update records on Mondays, and set time aside each Tuesday to wash the feed cups and water bottles. Keep pedigrees on all your breeding stock, write down mating and kindling dates immediately, and track your progress toward your goal.

Two Important Rabbit Managing Tips

Remember that one of the most important things you can do for your rabbits is simply to spend time with them. Take your homework out to the barn, or a book to read, and just sit for a while with your bunnies and observe their habits. By knowing their regular habits, you'll notice it quicker when something goes wrong, and you can often catch a minor problem before it becomes a major one.

Managing a rabbitry is a big job, and it's easy to get overwhelmed. So start small. Start with only ten cages and expand slowly as you learn. Stay in control; never let your rabbit project get so large that it controls you. Remember, a small ship with a rudder gets to its destination a lot faster than a big one that no one can steer.

Recommended Rabbitry Management Software:

Do yourself a favor and improve the efficiency of your rabbitry by utilizing these two pieces of easy to use rabbit software…

Rabbitry Management Software:

http://RabbitryManagementSoftware.com/

Via Premium Rabbits: http://www.premiumrabbits.com/easy-rabbitry-management-software/

Rabbit Pedigree Software:

http://RabbitPedigreeSoftware.com/

Via Premium Rabbits: http://www.premiumrabbits.com/easy-rabbit-pedigree-generator-2-0/

How to Handle a Rabbit

How to Handle a Rabbit. Discover the proper method that experienced rabbit owners use when handling rabbits in this article.

If you're a new bunny owner, you may find your pet a bit hard to handle at first. Don't worry, with practice you will catch on quickly. Until you get the hang of it, don't be ashamed to wear gloves and long sleeves. Bunnies aren't able to velvet their claws!

Handling a Rabbit: "Catch me if you can!"

Sometimes the most challenging part of handling a rabbit is simply getting it out of its rabbit cage! A rule of thumb is to always pull the bunny out of the cage tail-first. While this doesn't feel like the most natural way to go about handing rabbits, it is the safest. If your bunny gets used to jumping out of the cage into your arms, he may jump when you weren't ready and suffer a fall. You should place one hand on your rabbits' neck, lightly gripping his ears and the skin on the back of his shoulders. Do not pull him by the ears or skin; this hand is just there as a guide. Your other hand should go under his belly and do the lifting and pulling. Your bunny will find it harder to resist you if you draw him out tail-first. Be careful not to drag his toenails as they can break on the cage wire.

Make sure the Rabbit is Safe in Transit

Once you have the bunny out of the cage, the "football hold" is the best way to carry him from one place to another. If you removed the rabbit from the cage as described above, you already have your hands in the right position. Bring the rabbit under your arm so that his head is tucked between your arm and your side. The rabbit will be facing backwards and his weight will be resting on your arm. Make sure all four feet are supported; otherwise the rabbit may be frightened. This is the safest way to transport a rabbit; he is less likely to struggle if he can't see where he is going. If the rabbit tries to jump, you can quickly drop to one knee and secure him.

Examining a Rabbit

Although not always fun, it's important to take your bunny out and look him over regularly for signs of illness or injury. To do so, you will have to turn him upside-down. To accomplish this, place the rabbit on a table covered in carpet or another non-slip surface. Place one hand behind the ears and the other on his rump. Gently lift the rabbit by the base of the ears and the scruff of the neck, then scoop his rump with your other hand and turn him over. Again, the ears and skin behind the neck should only be held lightly as a guide; the real work is done by your hand on the bunny's rear. If your rabbit starts to struggle in this position, release him immediately, and then turn him back over once he is relaxed.

Handling a Rabbit: It's snuggle time!

When all you want is to have some one-on-one time with your bunny, there are a number of acceptable ways to handle him. Anything that works for you and the bun is probably okay, as long as you keep a few principles in mind:

-The rabbit's weight must always be supported by something firm under its body. Never use the ears, hips, or limbs to control a rabbit.
-Rabbits may be come frightened unless all four feet are resting on something solid.
-When you are standing, always hold a rabbit firmly, so that it cannot jump out of your arms if

suddenly frightened.

-Sitting on the floor or couch with the bunny on your lap is one of the best and safest ways to socialize.

Learn more about caring for your rabbits:

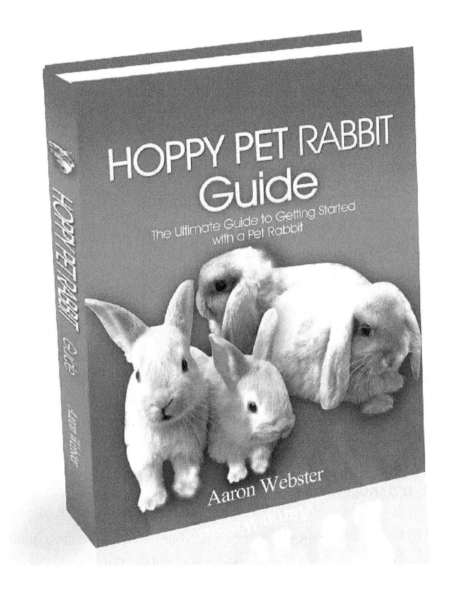

The Hoppy Pet Rabbit Guide:

http://www.premiumrabbits.com/hoppy-pet-rabbit-guide/

Via Amazon: http://rabbitbreeders.us/AmazonPetRabbits101

How to Groom a Rabbit

How to Groom a Rabbit. Find information about grooming rabbits for show. Grooming Do's and Don'ts listed.

The good news with regards to grooming rabbits is the fact that rabbits are naturally neat animals. They keep their own coats tidy with the help of their tiny built-in washcloths, their tongues. Certain short-haired rabbits may never need their owner to groom them. However, some breeds have long coats that require special care, and any bunny can occasionally get himself into trouble and want some hygiene help.

Grooming Short-haired Rabbits

The shorter a rabbit's coat, the less grooming it will require. Rex breeds have fur under an inch in length; it should never be brushed as this can damage the springy qualities of the coat.

Breeds with flyback fur, which is a little longer, do not usually require brushing. The only times they do might be during a molt, when brushing can help draw out dead fur. Before you put your bunny on the show table, you can moisten your hands with water and rub them back and forth through the coat to remove static and loose hairs. Breeds with flyback fur include Dutch, Polish, Californian, New Zealand, Tan, and several others.

Rollback fur is slightly longer than flyback fur. Many of the common breeds such as Holland Lops, Mini Lops, and Netherland Dwarfs have rollback fur. Rabbit Breeds with rollback coats can occasionally benefit from a going-over with a slicker brush, like the kind used for grooming dogs. Check the area around the tail and hind feet for matted fur or tangled debris. You can use the same trick with water on your hands that you use for flyback-coated breeds.

Grooming Rabbits with Long Wool

Some bunnies a long type of hair called wool. This can range from 2-3 inches on the Jersey Wooly to 4-10 inches on Angora breeds.

The Jersey Wooly and American Fuzzy Lop have short wool coats with a coarse texture. These are known as "easy care" coats, because they require much less grooming than full-length Angora wool. You should check these bunnies often to make sure they are not developing tangles. Remove any tangles or mats with a brush, comb, or nail scissors. Matting problems become especially evident during a molt. Other than that, they need little attention.

Angora rabbit coats need extensive care. They must be gently brushed as babies. On adult rabbits, many breeders use a blower, like a heatless hair dryer, to keep coats tangle free. Before you get an Angora, make sure to discuss grooming with the breeder you buy it from.

Removing Stains

Any rabbit can get stained, and bucks are particularly prone to it. A sticky, stained coat is very undesirable on the show table. You can quickly and easily remove stains by using a toothbrush to apply white alcohol or hydrogen peroxide, then sprinkling the area with cornstarch. Brush out the cornstarch the next day and you'll have a clean bunny.

How not to groom a rabbit

Except in extreme circumstances, you should never give your rabbit a full-blown bath. A full bath will damage the natural protective qualities in the coat. Also, you should never use grooming products or conditioners on your rabbits' coat. These count as unnatural "foreign substances" and can get your entire entry disqualified at an ARBA show.

How to Transport a Rabbit

How to Transport a Rabbit. In this article you will learn how to safely transport rabbits. Easy to understand step by step transporting instructions included.

The Right and the Wrong Reasons for Transporting a Rabbit

Before we talk about how to safely transport rabbits, let's consider why we are transporting them. Sometimes you definitely need to get a rabbit from one location to another, such as a sale or a trip to the vet. Breeders may take their animals to a show, or to the local library for a "bunny day" demo. All of these are fine reasons to transport bunnies. But should you take your rabbit on vacation with you?

Rabbits are "home bodies," as a rule. They don't prefer to travel far out of range from their cozy hole. While most rabbits do fine with one- or two-day excursions, they can become stressed by extended periods away from their home sweet homes. Therefore, for the bunny's sake, it's better to leave your rabbit behind when you go on vacation. Though there may be exceptions, rabbits in general will not enjoy traveling around town with you either, like a dog might. Extended travel can be dangerous for a small and flighty bunny.

The Safe Way to Travel with Rabbits

But as mentioned, there are some perfectly acceptable reasons to transport our furry friends. It can usually be done without accident when we take the right precautions. First, consider your carrier. The carrier should be much smaller than the rabbits' normal cage, without much room for the rabbit to move around. This will prevent the bunny from being slammed into the carrier wall if you make a sudden stop or turn. The carrier must have a floor of wire or some other grippy substance so your bunny can not slide around. You'll want to make sure the carrier or drop tray is bedded with an odor-absorbing material.

Position the carrier so that the rabbit is facing the side of your vehicle, rather than the front of it. That way, if you stop suddenly your rabbit's side will hit the carrier wall, not its face and teeth. Carriers must never be placed in the closed trunk of a car. Ideally, carriers should ride on the floor of your SUV or van, but they can also be placed in the covered back of a pickup truck if you make sure there is adequate ventilation, and frequently check to make sure the bunnies are not overheated. Fans should blow over carriers, not directly on them.

Feeding and Watering Rabbit while on the Road

Most rabbits will not eat while traveling. Do not place food or water dishes in the carriers, as they will spill and create a mess. It's much better to feed and water your bunnies once you arrive at your destination. During travel, place a fresh moist piece of apple or carrot in the carrier, which can be a source of both moisture and calories. Hay is also a good travel snack. You may want to offer a vitamin supplement such as Vita-Stress to offset the strain of transporting.

It's important to check your rabbits often during travel to make sure they are not overheated. After you arrive at your destination, check your bunny to make sure his teeth and toenails are intact and he's in good condition.

Find quality rabbit carriers for sale via: http://PremiumRabbits.com/

Preventing Sore Rabbit Hocks

Preventing Sore Rabbit Hocks – Learn how to prevent sore hocks in rabbits and how to treat rabbits with the condition in this article.

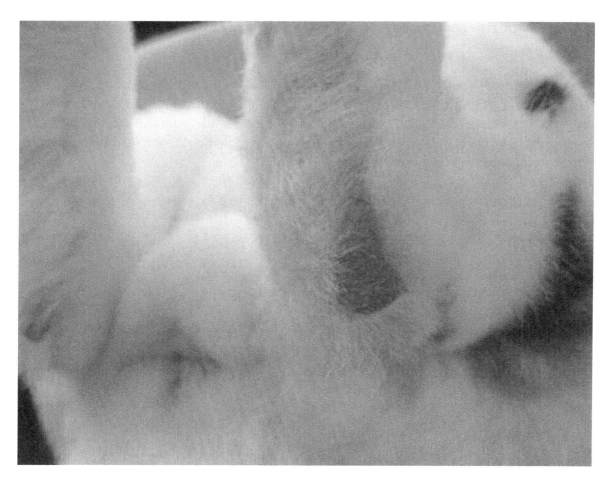

The other day my brother showed me some photos he had taken in the woods near our home. They were pictures of bear tracks. Black bear tracks. Yes, we live that far north.

One thing he pointed out in the photos was that some of the tracks were deeper than the others. Evidently bears rest more weight on their hind feed than they do on their front feet – just like rabbits. The back part of a rabbit's hind foot is called the hock, and this area supports most of the bunnyweight. The hock is normally covered with a thick layer of fuzz, but sometimes this fur wears away, and the skin on the hock can break and bleed. Average rabbit owners call this condition "sore hocks," though vets might term it pododermatitis or ulcerated foot pads. I'm not sure what you call it in bears.

Sore hocks can develop on any rabbit, but certain ones are more susceptible. Those would be the Rex-furred breeds (since they have short fine fur), the very large breeds (since they have more weight to bear), and excitable rabbits that stamp their feet a lot. It's also more common in rabbits that are housed in cages with wire floors. Put two of these factors together (i.e. rex fur + wire floor) and you will need to be proactive if you want to prevent "ouchie" bunny feet.

Unfortunately, once sore hocks have developed, they're very hard to treat. If the fur gets worn away, it will seldom grow back. Plus, since rabbits spend so much time on their feet, the skin doesn't have much of a chance to heal. So it's worth the trouble to institute a Pododermatitis Protection Plan.

That plan doesn't have to include moving your rabbits to solid-floored cages. I don't even recommend it. The reason why most rabbits are housed on wire floors is because wire floors are best for them. Cleanest. Safest. Healthiest. In fact, I read a study from the World Rabbit Council (summarized several years ago in Domestic Rabbits magazine) that said rabbits seemed to actually prefer wire floors if given the option.

So how can get all the benefits of a wire floor with none of the disadvantages?

Enter the EZ-Mat

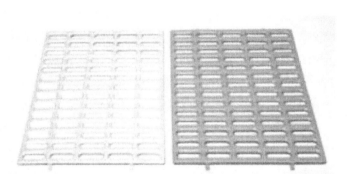

Plastic resting mats (also known as EZ-Mats) are extremely popular with rabbit owners, and for good reason. They're simply hard plastic mats – made of quality, non-toxic ABS – that lay over the top of the cage floor, giving your rabbit a place to rest off the wire. They have very smooth surfaces; all the edges are carefully beveled to prevent wear on your rabbit's feet. And they are super sanitary. They have slots punched out that allow waste to fall right through into the drop pan. And if the mats ever get dirty, they're easy to wash with soap and water. You can even put them in your dishwasher! (My family has never been cool with that idea, though.)

Ask around to your bunny friends, and you'll probably find that most of them use resting mats. If you don't have any yet for your bunnies, today is a great day to go EZ-Mat shopping, because a popular rabbit supply company is offering a sale on EZ-Mats right now.

Sale on EZ-Mats

Follow the below links to save money on EZ-Mats from PremiumRabbits.com.

Individual: http://www.premiumrabbits.com/ez-mat-cage-floor-mat/
Pack of Twelve: http://www.premiumrabbits.com/ez-mat-cage-floor-mat-pack-of-twelve/

While you're at PremiumRabbits.com, check out the other supplies we offer: cages, carriers, nest boxes, dishes, toys, and lots more. If you have any questions while you're there, just call 1-800-809-8752 or sign into live chat. We'll be happy to help!

But wait, has your rabbit already developed sore hocks?

If your rabbit already has sore hocks, resting mats can definitely help. Additionally we recommend that you apply some Bunny Balm (also used during rabbit tattooing) on the sore area to help get rid of the condition. I personally apply the KBtatts All Natural Bunny Balm when my rabbits get sore hocks.

You can grab some for use via:
http://www.premiumrabbits.com/kbtatts-bunny-balm/ .

Understanding Rabbit Pedigrees

Rabbit Pedigrees. In this article we will be discussing the subject of rabbit pedigrees and I will provide you with tips for creating your own.

What is a rabbit pedigree?

All rabbits have ancestors, right? But not all rabbits have pedigrees. A pedigree is simply a record of a rabbit's ancestors. If you have a document that lists your rabbit's parents, grand-parents, and great-grandparents, your bunny is fully pedigreed.

A pedigreed rabbit is not necessarily the same as a purebred rabbit. Any rabbit can have a pedigree, even if it comes from a mixed lineage. A purebred rabbit has at least three generations of ancestors of only one breed. If you lose the pedigree on your purebred rabbit, it's still a purebred. Both terms are also different from the term "registered." A registered rabbit is a purebred that has a full pedigree, and that has been officially been filed into the records of the American Rabbit Breeders Association. A registered rabbit must have a full purebred pedigree, but a rabbit may be a purebred and have a pedigree, but still not be registered.

How do I produce a pedigree for my rabbits?

Only a licensed registrar can register your rabbit with the ARBA, but any breeder can make an official pedigree for the babies they produce. If both parents are pedigreed, you have all the information you need to make a pedigree for the babies. There are several ways to produce a pedigree. You can order pedigree blanks from some cage suppliers. If you're good with the computer, you can produce your own using Microsoft Word or a similar program. You can Google "custom rabbit pedigree designs" to find companies that offer this service. Or you can purchase rabbitry management software such as The Easy Rabbit Pedigree Generator which we recommend to help aid you in the pedigree data storage and generation process.

Learn more about The Easy Rabbit Pedigree Generator:
http://rabbitbreeders.us/newsletter/rabbit-pedigree-software/

What information does a rabbit pedigree contain?

The pedigrees you provide for the bunnies you sell should contain all the information that people need to register their rabbits with the ARBA if they so choose. In order to be ARBA registered, a rabbit must have a pedigree that contains the following information on the bunny itself and three generations of its ancestors, i.e. its parents, grandparents, and great grandparents.

-Name – Breeders can name their rabbits anything they like. Most breeders use a prefix before the rabbit's name to indicate the breeder, such as Katie's Fluffy, Jones' Cookies, or BTR's Bucky.

– Color – This is the registration variety; the exact color of the bunny. Write "broken blue" instead of just "broken" or "blue tortoise" instead of just "tort."
– Ear Number – this is the tattoo found in the left ear of the rabbit.
– Weight – Weights on rabbits' pedigrees are written with a decimal point, however, weights are not written in the metric system. Instead, the number 4.5 would indicate four pounds and five ounces, not four and a half.
-Registration and Grand Championship numbers – Provide these ARBA numbers when applicable.
That's all the info that pedigrees must have, however, breeders often like to provide a few more details. Optional information includes winnings, number of Grand Championship legs, genotype, ear length, and additional generations of ancestors.

Rabbit Resources

Here is a listing of some awesome rabbit resources that I recommend that you at least checkout... (Listings include rabbit suppliers/vendors, rabbit products + websites and various rabbit related clubs/organizations)

Rabbit Suppliers/Vendors: General Supplies

Resource #1: PremiumRabbits.com

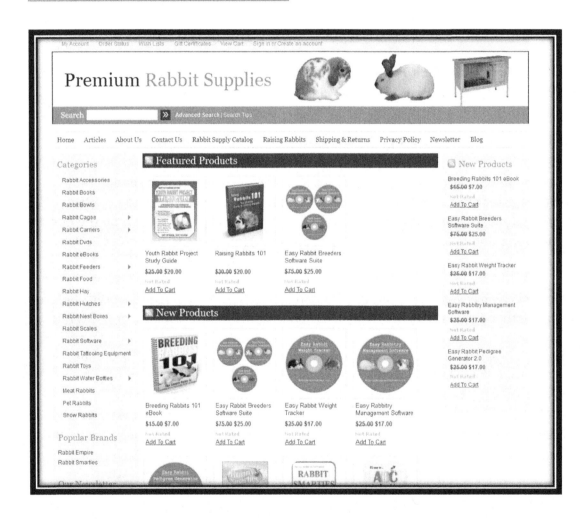

Description: If you are looking to purchase quality rabbit supplies at affordable prices I highly recommend that you checkout PremiumRabbits.com. (My number #1 Rabbit Supplier Recommendation)

URL: http://premiumrabbits.com/

Raising Rabbits 101 – The Ultimate Guide to Raising Rabbits

Rabbit Suppliers/Vendors: General Supplies

Resource #2: Amazon

Description: Surprisingly enough you can find many of the rabbit supplies that we recommend throughout this book directly on the Amazon website. Also Amazon helps us out by selling this book and other products produced by us on their website. So if you are interested in buying supplies and would like to search on Amazon, be sure to click the link below to secure your special pricing and deals on various products.

URL: http://rabbitbreeders.us/amazon

Rabbit Products: Books/Reports

Resource #3: Raising Meat Pen Rabbits

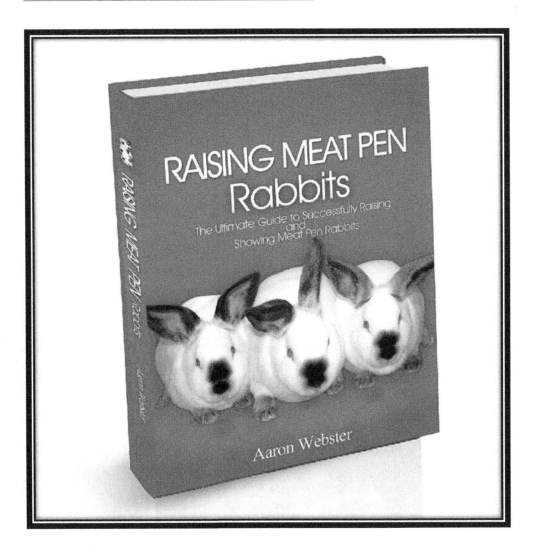

Description: If you are interested in raising and showing meat pen rabbits, this is the book for you. Available for purchase via PremiumRabbits.com and Amazon.com you can grab a copy of this exclusive report in both eBook and Softcover Book format. Within the book you will learn all about the meat pen rabbit showing industry and will be walked through the process of raising meat pen rabbits for show. This book was written specifically with the 4-H and FFA student in mind.

URL: http://www.premiumrabbits.com/raising-meat-pen-rabbits/

Via Amazon: http://rabbitbreeders.us/AmazonMeatPenRabbits

Rabbit Products: Books/Reports

Resource #4: Hoppy Pet Rabbit Guide

Description: If you are interested in owning a pet rabbit this is definitely the book for you. Within the Hoppy Pet Rabbit Guide you will learn all about how to successfully care for a pet rabbit. This book was written with the specific purpose of helping newbies get started with owning an indoor pet rabbit. This book is very kid friendly and filled with adorable rabbit pictures and interviews with other pet rabbit owners.

URL: http://www.premiumrabbits.com/hoppy-pet-rabbit-guide/

Via Amazon: http://rabbitbreeders.us/AmazonPetRabbits101

Rabbit Products: Books/Reports

Resource #5: The Youth Rabbit Project Study Guide

Description: If you are interested in getting involved in the rabbit showing industry, I highly recommend that you grab yourself a copy of The Youth Rabbit Project Study Guide written by Ellyn from Rabbit Smarties. The book is filled with information that will help you better understand the rabbit showing industry and potentially even participate in a rabbit showmanship competition.

URL: http://www.premiumrabbits.com/youth-rabbit-project-study-guide/

Rabbit Products: Books/Reports

Resource #6: The Rabbit Coat Color Genetics Guide

Description: Are you interested in learning more about rabbit coat color genetics? If you are I recommend that you grab yourself a copy of a new book written by Ellyn from Rabbit Smarties on that specific topic. Within the Rabbit Coat Colors Genetics Guide you will learn all about the in-depth subject of bunny colors and how to breed for certain ones.

URL: http://www.premiumrabbits.com/the-rabbit-coat-colors-genetics-guide/

Rabbit Products: Software for Rabbit Raisers

Resource #7: The Easy Rabbitry Management Software

Description: If you are looking to find an easy to use software solution that will help you manage all your rabbitry records, The Easy Rabbitry Management Software is the ideal software solution for you. The program easily and effectively helps you manage and store all your rabbitry records in minutes after installation. No learning curve required...

URL: http://RabbitryManagementSoftware.com/

Rabbit Products: Software for Rabbit Raisers

Resource #8: The Easy Rabbit Pedigree Software

Description: If you are looking to find an easy to use software solution that will allow you to easily create your own rabbit pedigrees and that doesn't cost a fortune, The Easy Rabbit Pedigree Software is the program for you. The program is simple to use and is available for a much lower price than many of the other pedigree creation programs available on the market.

URL: http://RabbitPedigreeSoftware.com/

Rabbit Websites: Membership sites for Rabbit Raisers

Resource #9: TheRabbitMentor.com

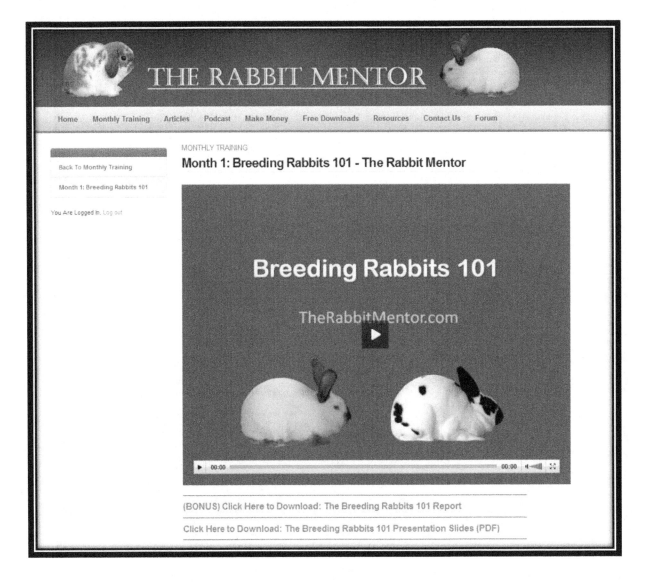

Description: Out of all the rabbit resources that I recommend within this book, The Rabbit Mentor is probably my personal favorite. Essentially The Rabbit Mentor is a training program for rabbit raisers, setup in a way that you will receive monthly training videos on the different aspects of your rabbit project (ranging from Breeding to Feeding to Housing to Marketing, etc). Normally the training program/membership website would cost $10/month however currently a MEGA discount is being offered on the program that will enable you to gain lifetime access for a ridiculously low onetime fee. Visit TheRabbitMentor.com to learn more...

URL: http://therabbitmentor.com/

Rabbit Websites: Membership sites for Rabbit Raisers

Resource #10: SellRabbitsOnDemand.com

Description: As I have mentioned before, one of the most important things that will determine the success of your rabbitry is your ability to essentially "sell your rabbits on demand". As a member of this exclusive new "industry changing" membership website (created by the author of this book)... you will be given access to a system that will essentially allow you to start selling your rabbits on demand. Basically as a member of the Sell Rabbits On Demand site you will be able to post virtually unlimited rabbit classifieds on our high traffic + targeted rabbit website network, including but not limited to RabbitBreeders.us (which by itself has received over 5 million visits). Lifetime membership to the program is currently being offered at huge discount.

URL: http://sellrabbitsondemand.com/

Raising Rabbits 101 – *The Ultimate Guide to Raising Rabbits*

page 156

Rabbit Websites: Information/Resources

Resource #11: RabbitBreeders.us

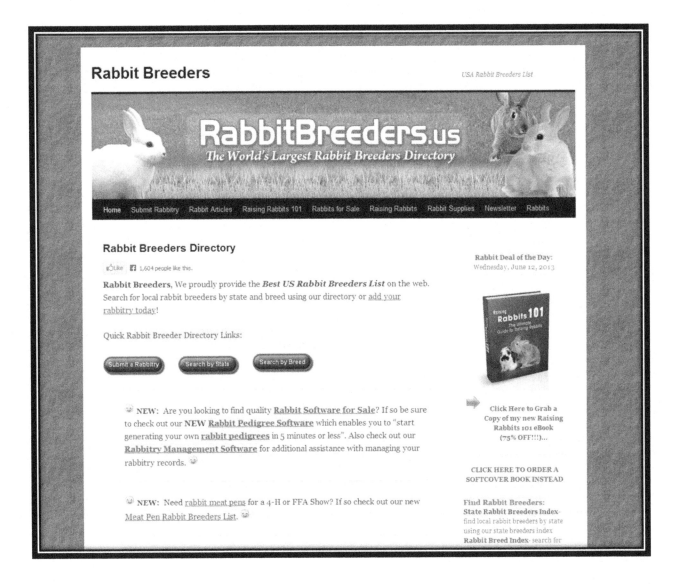

Description: If you are looking to find rabbits for sale in your area, RabbitBreeders.us is definitely the site that you want to check out. At RabbitBreeders.us you can browse a directory of over 2,500 rabbitries (and growing) to locate rabbit breeders in any of the 50 states. Also we have setup two sister site directories for Canada and England which can now be located on RabbitBreeders.us. If you have a rabbitry of your own… feel free to submit it to our directory (free of charge) as well.

URL: http://rabbitbreeders.us/

Raising Rabbits 101 4th Edition – Copyright © 2015

Rabbit Websites: Information/Resources

Resource #12: RaisingRabbitsBlog.com

Description: RaisingRabbitsBlog.com is currently one of the leading rabbit blog sites online started by us here at Rabbit Empire. You can go here to find additional rabbit information and articles on subjects such as raising rabbits for FFA, owning a pet rabbit, rabbit tattooing, general rabbit care and more.

URL: http://raisingrabbitsblog.com/

Rabbit Club/Organization Listings:

Resource #13: ARBA

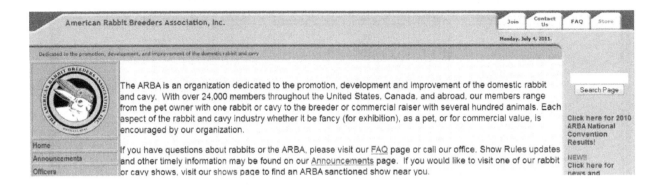

Description: American Rabbit Breeders Association – the largest rabbit breeders' organization in the World. (Currently has over 20,000 members)

URL: http://www.arba.net/

Resource #14: British Rabbit Council

Description: The British Rabbit Council is the largest rabbit organization and club in the UK.

URL: http://www.thebrc.org/

Final Words:

Great happiness and satisfaction may be waiting for you to make the initial step and get your hands wet in the growing rabbit industry! Hopefully with the information inside this book at your disposal you will be able to turn your rabbit experiment into a success...

First off I hope you enjoyed reading this 4th Edition of Raising Rabbits 101. I would appreciate it if you would take a few minutes to email me feedback at support@rabbitbreeders.us. Please send me your honest opinions about this book.

Please note: This is an ever growing and improving book. I hope to be able to make each future edition of this book better than the previous one. To help me do this; be sure to include topic suggestions in the feedback email.

Special Contest

Photos: Currently we are having a little contest to help gather rabbit breed photos for our website breed gallery and for future informational articles. If you would like to have a chance to make your beloved rabbit famous and to win some really cool prizes, feel free to participate. You can send your rabbit photos to me via email - (support@rabbitbreeders.us). Note: Please be sure to include your name and the breed of rabbit that is in the picture, somewhere inside of the email along with a short photo description.

View our current Rabbit Photo Contest Gallery: http://rabbitbreeders.us/pictures-of-rabbits

Stories: In addition to hosting the rabbit photo contest we thought that it would be interesting to arrange a rabbit story contest. This is a chance for you to win prizes by submitting a cute, sad, funny or flat out hilarious rabbit story. Share those rabbit memories: support@rabbitbreeders.us (please type up stories in a Microsoft Word Document)

Spread the Word

If you enjoyed this book... why not let some of your other rabbit friends know about it? Take a few moments to help us spread the word by doing one of the following things; tell a friend about our book, link to our main website RabbitBreeders.us on your website if you have one, or simply become a fan of our Popular Rabbit Breeders Facebook Page: https://www.facebook.com/USARabbitBreeders .

Happy Rabbit Raising + Talk Soon!

Sincerely,
Aaron "The Rabbit Master" Webster

P.S: Be sure to check out the bonus section of this book! (Part 7)

Enjoy Raising Rabbits 101?
Why not check out our other recently published titles?

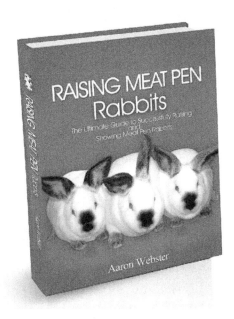 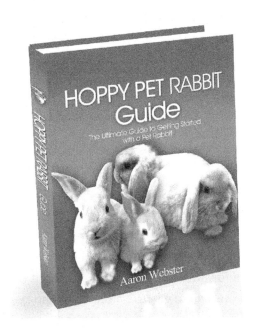

#1: Raising Meat Pen Rabbits

"The Ultimate Guide to Successfully Raising and Showing Meat Pen Rabbits"

Via Premium Rabbits: http://www.premiumrabbits.com/raising-meat-pen-rabbits/

Via Amazon: http://rabbitbreeders.us/AmazonMeatPenRabbits

#2: Hoppy Pet Rabbit Guide

"The Ultimate Guide to Getting Started with a Pet Rabbit"

Via Premium Rabbits: http://www.premiumrabbits.com/hoppy-pet-rabbit-guide/

Via Amazon: http://rabbitbreeders.us/AmazonPetRabbits101

Part 7: Bonus Section and Glossary

Rabbit Breeding Calendar

When will my bunnies be born? When does my doe need a nest box?

Date Bred	Date to Add Nest Box	Predicted Day of Birth
<u>January</u>		
1-Jan	28-Jan	31-Jan
2-Jan	29-Jan	1-Feb
3-Jan	30-Jan	2-Feb
4-Jan	31-Jan	3-Feb
5-Jan	1-Feb	4-Feb
6-Jan	2-Feb	5-Feb
7-Jan	3-Feb	6-Feb
8-Jan	4-Feb	7-Feb
9-Jan	5-Feb	8-Feb
10-Jan	6-Feb	9-Feb
11-Jan	7-Feb	10-Feb
12-Jan	8-Feb	11-Feb
13-Jan	9-Feb	12-Feb
14-Jan	10-Feb	13-Feb
15-Jan	11-Feb	14-Feb
16-Jan	12-Feb	15-Feb
17-Jan	13-Feb	16-Feb
18-Jan	14-Feb	17-Feb
19-Jan	15-Feb	18-Feb
20-Jan	16-Feb	19-Feb
21-Jan	17-Feb	20-Feb
22-Jan	18-Feb	21-Feb
23-Jan	19-Feb	22-Feb
24-Jan	20-Feb	23-Feb
25-Jan	21-Feb	24-Feb
26-Jan	22-Feb	25-Feb
27-Jan	23-Feb	26-Feb
28-Jan	24-Feb	27-Feb
29-Jan	25-Feb	28-Feb
30-Jan	26-Feb	1-Mar
31-Jan	27-Feb	2-Mar
<u>February</u>		
1-Feb	28-Feb	3-Mar
2-Feb	1-Mar	4-Mar
3-Feb	2-Mar	5-Mar
4-Feb	3-Mar	6-Mar
5-Feb	4-Mar	7-Mar
6-Feb	5-Mar	8-Mar
7-Feb	6-Mar	9-Mar
8-Feb	7-Mar	10-Mar
9-Feb	8-Mar	11-Mar
10-Feb	9-Mar	12-Mar
11-Feb	10-Mar	13-Mar

Raising Rabbits 101 4th Edition – Copyright © 2015

12-Feb	11-Mar	14-Mar
13-Feb	12-Mar	15-Mar
14-Feb	13-Mar	16-Mar
15-Feb	14-Mar	17-Mar
16-Feb	15-Mar	18-Mar
17-Feb	16-Mar	19-Mar
18-Feb	17-Mar	20-Mar
19-Feb	18-Mar	21-Mar
20-Feb	19-Mar	22-Mar
21-Feb	20-Mar	23-Mar
22-Feb	21-Mar	24-Mar
23-Feb	22-Mar	25-Mar
24-Feb	23-Mar	26-Mar
25-Feb	24-Mar	27-Mar
26-Feb	25-Mar	28-Mar
27-Feb	26-Mar	29-Mar
28-Feb	27-Mar	30-Mar
	March	
1-Mar	28-Mar	31-Mar
2-Mar	29-Mar	1-Apr
3-Mar	30-Mar	2-Apr
4-Mar	31-Mar	3-Apr
5-Mar	1-Apr	4-Apr
6-Mar	2-Apr	5-Apr
7-Mar	3-Apr	6-Apr
8-Mar	4-Apr	7-Apr
9-Mar	5-Apr	8-Apr
10-Mar	6-Apr	9-Apr
11-Mar	7-Apr	10-Apr
12-Mar	8-Apr	11-Apr
13-Mar	9-Apr	12-Apr
14-Mar	10-Apr	13-Apr
15-Mar	11-Apr	14-Apr
16-Mar	12-Apr	15-Apr
17-Mar	13-Apr	16-Apr
18-Mar	14-Apr	17-Apr
19-Mar	15-Apr	18-Apr
20-Mar	16-Apr	19-Apr
21-Mar	17-Apr	20-Apr
22-Mar	18-Apr	21-Apr
23-Mar	19-Apr	22-Apr
24-Mar	20-Apr	23-Apr
25-Mar	21-Apr	24-Apr
26-Mar	22-Apr	25-Apr
27-Mar	23-Apr	26-Apr
28-Mar	24-Apr	27-Apr
29-Mar	25-Apr	28-Apr
30-Mar	26-Apr	29-Apr
31-Mar	27-Apr	30-Apr
	April	

1-Apr	28-Apr	1-May
2-Apr	29-Apr	2-May
3-Apr	30-Apr	3-May
4-Apr	1-May	4-May
5-Apr	2-May	5-May
6-Apr	3-May	6-May
7-Apr	4-May	7-May
8-Apr	5-May	8-May
9-Apr	6-May	9-May
10-Apr	7-May	10-May
11-Apr	8-May	11-May
12-Apr	9-May	12-May
13-Apr	10-May	13-May
14-Apr	11-May	14-May
15-Apr	12-May	15-May
16-Apr	13-May	16-May
17-Apr	14-May	17-May
18-Apr	15-May	18-May
19-Apr	16-May	19-May
20-Apr	17-May	20-May
21-Apr	18-May	21-May
22-Apr	19-May	22-May
23-Apr	20-May	23-May
24-Apr	21-May	24-May
25-Apr	22-May	25-May
26-Apr	23-May	26-May
27-Apr	24-May	27-May
28-Apr	25-May	28-May
29-Apr	26-May	29-May
30-Apr	27-May	30-May
May		
1-May	28-May	31-May
2-May	29-May	1-Jun
3-May	30-May	2-Jun
4-May	31-May	3-Jun
5-May	1-Jun	4-Jun
6-May	2-Jun	5-Jun
7-May	3-Jun	6-Jun
8-May	4-Jun	7-Jun
9-May	5-Jun	8-Jun
10-May	6-Jun	9-Jun
11-May	7-Jun	10-Jun
12-May	8-Jun	11-Jun
13-May	9-Jun	12-Jun
14-May	10-Jun	13-Jun
15-May	11-Jun	14-Jun
16-May	12-Jun	15-Jun
17-May	13-Jun	16-Jun
18-May	14-Jun	17-Jun
19-May	15-Jun	18-Jun

20-May	16-Jun	19-Jun
21-May	17-Jun	20-Jun
22-May	18-Jun	21-Jun
23-May	19-Jun	22-Jun
24-May	20-Jun	23-Jun
25-May	21-Jun	24-Jun
26-May	22-Jun	25-Jun
27-May	23-Jun	26-Jun
28-May	24-Jun	27-Jun
29-May	25-Jun	28-Jun
30-May	26-Jun	29-Jun
31-May	27-Jun	30-Jun
<u>June</u>		
1-Jun	28-Jun	1-Jul
2-Jun	29-Jun	2-Jul
3-Jun	30-Jun	3-Jul
4-Jun	1-Jul	4-Jul
5-Jun	2-Jul	5-Jul
6-Jun	3-Jul	6-Jul
7-Jun	4-Jul	7-Jul
8-Jun	5-Jul	8-Jul
9-Jun	6-Jul	9-Jul
10-Jun	7-Jul	10-Jul
11-Jun	8-Jul	11-Jul
12-Jun	9-Jul	12-Jul
13-Jun	10-Jul	13-Jul
14-Jun	11-Jul	14-Jul
15-Jun	12-Jul	15-Jul
16-Jun	13-Jul	16-Jul
17-Jun	14-Jul	17-Jul
18-Jun	15-Jul	18-Jul
19-Jun	16-Jul	19-Jul
20-Jun	17-Jul	20-Jul
21-Jun	18-Jul	21-Jul
22-Jun	19-Jul	22-Jul
23-Jun	20-Jul	23-Jul
24-Jun	21-Jul	24-Jul
25-Jun	22-Jul	25-Jul
26-Jun	23-Jul	26-Jul
27-Jun	24-Jul	27-Jul
28-Jun	25-Jul	28-Jul
29-Jun	26-Jul	29-Jul
30-Jun	27-Jul	30-Jul
<u>July</u>		
1-Jul	28-Jul	31-Jul
2-Jul	29-Jul	1-Aug
3-Jul	30-Jul	2-Aug
4-Jul	31-Jul	3-Aug
5-Jul	1-Aug	4-Aug
6-Jul	2-Aug	5-Aug

7-Jul	3-Aug	6-Aug
8-Jul	4-Aug	7-Aug
9-Jul	5-Aug	8-Aug
10-Jul	6-Aug	9-Aug
11-Jul	7-Aug	10-Aug
12-Jul	8-Aug	11-Aug
13-Jul	9-Aug	12-Aug
14-Jul	10-Aug	13-Aug
15-Jul	11-Aug	14-Aug
16-Jul	12-Aug	15-Aug
17-Jul	13-Aug	16-Aug
18-Jul	14-Aug	17-Aug
19-Jul	15-Aug	18-Aug
20-Jul	16-Aug	19-Aug
21-Jul	17-Aug	20-Aug
22-Jul	18-Aug	21-Aug
23-Jul	19-Aug	22-Aug
24-Jul	20-Aug	23-Aug
25-Jul	21-Aug	24-Aug
26-Jul	22-Aug	25-Aug
27-Jul	23-Aug	26-Aug
28-Jul	24-Aug	27-Aug
29-Jul	25-Aug	28-Aug
30-Jul	26-Aug	29-Aug
31-Jul	27-Aug	30-Aug
August		
1-Aug	28-Aug	31-Aug
2-Aug	29-Aug	1-Sep
3-Aug	30-Aug	2-Sep
4-Aug	31-Aug	3-Sep
5-Aug	1-Sep	4-Sep
6-Aug	2-Sep	5-Sep
7-Aug	3-Sep	6-Sep
8-Aug	4-Sep	7-Sep
9-Aug	5-Sep	8-Sep
10-Aug	6-Sep	9-Sep
11-Aug	7-Sep	10-Sep
12-Aug	8-Sep	11-Sep
13-Aug	9-Sep	12-Sep
14-Aug	10-Sep	13-Sep
15-Aug	11-Sep	14-Sep
16-Aug	12-Sep	15-Sep
17-Aug	13-Sep	16-Sep
18-Aug	14-Sep	17-Sep
19-Aug	15-Sep	18-Sep
20-Aug	16-Sep	19-Sep
21-Aug	17-Sep	20-Sep
22-Aug	18-Sep	21-Sep
23-Aug	19-Sep	22-Sep
24-Aug	20-Sep	23-Sep

25-Aug	21-Sep	24-Sep
26-Aug	22-Sep	25-Sep
27-Aug	23-Sep	26-Sep
28-Aug	24-Sep	27-Sep
29-Aug	25-Sep	28-Sep
30-Aug	26-Sep	29-Sep
31-Aug	27-Sep	30-Sep
	September	
1-Sep	28-Sep	1-Oct
2-Sep	29-Sep	2-Oct
3-Sep	30-Sep	3-Oct
4-Sep	1-Oct	4-Oct
5-Sep	2-Oct	5-Oct
6-Sep	3-Oct	6-Oct
7-Sep	4-Oct	7-Oct
8-Sep	5-Oct	8-Oct
9-Sep	6-Oct	9-Oct
10-Sep	7-Oct	10-Oct
11-Sep	8-Oct	11-Oct
12-Sep	9-Oct	12-Oct
13-Sep	10-Oct	13-Oct
14-Sep	11-Oct	14-Oct
15-Sep	12-Oct	15-Oct
16-Sep	13-Oct	16-Oct
17-Sep	14-Oct	17-Oct
18-Sep	15-Oct	18-Oct
19-Sep	16-Oct	19-Oct
20-Sep	17-Oct	20-Oct
21-Sep	18-Oct	21-Oct
22-Sep	19-Oct	22-Oct
23-Sep	20-Oct	23-Oct
24-Sep	21-Oct	24-Oct
25-Sep	22-Oct	25-Oct
26-Sep	23-Oct	26-Oct
27-Sep	24-Oct	27-Oct
28-Sep	25-Oct	28-Oct
29-Sep	26-Oct	29-Oct
30-Sep	27-Oct	30-Oct
	October	
1-Oct	28-Oct	31-Oct
2-Oct	29-Oct	1-Nov
3-Oct	30-Oct	2-Nov
4-Oct	31-Oct	3-Nov
5-Oct	1-Nov	4-Nov
6-Oct	2-Nov	5-Nov
7-Oct	3-Nov	6-Nov
8-Oct	4-Nov	7-Nov
9-Oct	5-Nov	8-Nov
10-Oct	6-Nov	9-Nov
11-Oct	7-Nov	10-Nov

12-Oct	8-Nov	11-Nov
13-Oct	9-Nov	12-Nov
14-Oct	10-Nov	13-Nov
15-Oct	11-Nov	14-Nov
16-Oct	12-Nov	15-Nov
17-Oct	13-Nov	16-Nov
18-Oct	14-Nov	17-Nov
19-Oct	15-Nov	18-Nov
20-Oct	16-Nov	19-Nov
21-Oct	17-Nov	20-Nov
22-Oct	18-Nov	21-Nov
23-Oct	19-Nov	22-Nov
24-Oct	20-Nov	23-Nov
25-Oct	21-Nov	24-Nov
26-Oct	22-Nov	25-Nov
27-Oct	23-Nov	26-Nov
28-Oct	24-Nov	27-Nov
29-Oct	25-Nov	28-Nov
30-Oct	26-Nov	29-Nov
31-Oct	27-Nov	30-Nov
November		
1-Nov	28-Nov	1-Dec
2-Nov	29-Nov	2-Dec
3-Nov	30-Nov	3-Dec
4-Nov	1-Dec	4-Dec
5-Nov	2-Dec	5-Dec
6-Nov	3-Dec	6-Dec
7-Nov	4-Dec	7-Dec
8-Nov	5-Dec	8-Dec
9-Nov	6-Dec	9-Dec
10-Nov	7-Dec	10-Dec
11-Nov	8-Dec	11-Dec
12-Nov	9-Dec	12-Dec
13-Nov	10-Dec	13-Dec
14-Nov	11-Dec	14-Dec
15-Nov	12-Dec	15-Dec
16-Nov	13-Dec	16-Dec
17-Nov	14-Dec	17-Dec
18-Nov	15-Dec	18-Dec
19-Nov	16-Dec	19-Dec
20-Nov	17-Dec	20-Dec
21-Nov	18-Dec	21-Dec
22-Nov	19-Dec	22-Dec
23-Nov	20-Dec	23-Dec
24-Nov	21-Dec	24-Dec
25-Nov	22-Dec	25-Dec
26-Nov	23-Dec	26-Dec
27-Nov	24-Dec	27-Dec
28-Nov	25-Dec	28-Dec
29-Nov	26-Dec	29-Dec

30-Nov	27-Dec	30-Dec
December		
1-Dec	28-Dec	31-Dec
2-Dec	29-Dec	1-Jan
3-Dec	30-Dec	2-Jan
4-Dec	31-Dec	3-Jan
5-Dec	1-Jan	4-Jan
6-Dec	2-Jan	5-Jan
7-Dec	3-Jan	6-Jan
8-Dec	4-Jan	7-Jan
9-Dec	5-Jan	8-Jan
10-Dec	6-Jan	9-Jan
11-Dec	7-Jan	10-Jan
12-Dec	8-Jan	11-Jan
13-Dec	9-Jan	12-Jan
14-Dec	10-Jan	13-Jan
15-Dec	11-Jan	14-Jan
16-Dec	12-Jan	15-Jan
17-Dec	13-Jan	16-Jan
18-Dec	14-Jan	17-Jan
19-Dec	15-Jan	18-Jan
20-Dec	16-Jan	19-Jan
21-Dec	17-Jan	20-Jan
22-Dec	18-Jan	21-Jan
23-Dec	19-Jan	22-Jan
24-Dec	20-Jan	23-Jan
25-Dec	21-Jan	24-Jan
26-Dec	22-Jan	25-Jan
27-Dec	23-Jan	26-Jan
28-Dec	24-Jan	27-Jan
29-Dec	25-Jan	28-Jan
30-Dec	26-Jan	29-Jan
31-Dec	27-Jan	30-Jan

Bonus: Rabbitry Interviews

Learn from other successful rabbitry owners. This special bonus pdf that I assembled a couple years ago titled "Rabbitry Interviews 2011" contains interviews with 10 featured rabbitry owners. You can download it for free using the below link.

Download link: http://rabbitbreeders.us/rabbitry-interviews-pdf

Bonus: Rabbit Names List

Looking for rabbit name ideas? Download our huge list of rabbit name ideas via this link: http://RabbitBreeders.us/NameIdeasPDF .

A-Z Rabbit Names List - Bunny Rabbit Name Ideas

Boy Rabbit Names

A

Aaron
Abba
Abban
Abbott
Abe
Abel
Abhay
Abhi
Abie
Abiel
Ace
Achilles
Adam
Addison
Adel
Aden
Adonis
Adrian
Ajax
Andrew
Arthur
Austin
Avan
Azi

B

Bailey
Baird
Barber
Bardo
Barnabas
Barney
Basil
Bill
Bing
Birch
Bishop
Blaz
Bo
Boaz
Booth
Boris
Bowie
Blad
Brae
Buckley
Burr
Buster

C

Cable
Cadeo
Caesar
Cahil
Cain
Cal
Calvin
Cam
Capulet
Carl
Carson
Casper
Cecil
Charles
Chas
Chase
Chen
Cherokee
Chester
Chevy
Chico
Chuck
Cliff
Clovis
Conroy
Cosmo
Curt
Cyrus

D

Dacey
Dali
Daku
Dallas
Dallin
Damen
Darius
Darwin
Davey
Delano
Des
Devi
Dexter
Dian
Dick
Dickie
Diego
Dino
Dodd
Donald
Duff
Dwane

E

Earl
Earvin
Eban
Eddie
Elan
Elias

Rabbit Glossary

List of terms and abbreviations pertaining to rabbits - next page contains definitions

Abscess	Dam	Line Breeding
Adult	Dewlap	Litter
Albino	Doe	Live Weight
ARBA	Domestic Rabbit	Lop
Arch	DQ	Malocclusion
Back	Ear Canker	Market Age
Balanced	Embryo	Molting
Bangs	Entry	Mortality
Bare Spot	Faking	Muzzle
Belly	Faults	Nationals
BIS	Feces	Nest box
Bloodline	Fertility	Open Show
BOB	Finish	Out Breeding
BOS	Flesh Condition	Ovulation
BOSV	Foot	Pair
BOV	Forehead	Palpation
Breeder	Forequarters	Parasite
BRC	Fostering	Pathogen
Breeding Certificate	Fryer	Peanut
BRIS	Genotype	Pedigree
Broken	Gestation	Phenotype
Buck	Grand Champion	Processing
Buck-Teeth	Guard Hair	Rabbit Cage
Bunny Box	Hormone	Rabbit Hutch
Bull Dog	Hindquarters	Rabbitry
Cannibalism	Hip	Registrar
Carcass	Hock	Registration
Carcass Weight	HRS	Rex
Carriage	Inbreeding	Ribs
Cheek	Incisors	Sanctioned
Chest	Inherited	Senior
Chopped	Inner Ear	Service
Choppy	Insemination	Shoulders
Class	Intermediate	Sire
Classification	Inventory	Snuffles
Cobby	Junior	Symmetry
Cold	Kindling	Tattoo
Convention	Kit	Trio
Crossbred	Kittens	Uterus
Crossbreeding	Knee	Variety
Crown	Lactation	Weaning
Cull	Lapin	Wolf Teeth
Culling	Legs	Youth Exhibitor

Rabbit Terms and Definitions

A

Abscess- a lump on a rabbit's skin which is hard and filled with pus

Adult- in most rabbit breed shows which have four main breed classes, an adult rabbit is considered to be a rabbit that is at least six months of age or older

Albino- a rabbit which has white hair and pink eyes

ARBA- acronym for the American Rabbit Breeders Association

Arch- the curvature of a rabbit's spine, which starts on the neck or shoulders and extends to the rear of the rabbit

B

Back- the portion of a rabbit which extends from the neck to the tail

Balanced- a rabbit which has an "equal" distribution of meat and flesh across its body, used to describe a show or meat rabbit

Bangs- the long wool which appears at the front base of the ears and top of the head in some rabbit breeds

Bare Spot- any portion on a rabbit's pelt that lacks fur due to a molt, fur mites or another cause

Belly- the lower section of a rabbit's body which contains the abdomen and intestines

BIS- acronym for Best in Show- the rabbit of any breed that is judged to be the "best" bunny at a show

Bloodline- a term used to describe the ancestry of a given rabbit or herd; usually in terms of physical and genetic makeup (Example: This rabbit came from Joe Jone's winning bloodline!)

BOB- acronym for Best of Breed- rabbit that is selected to be the "best" rabbit of any given breed at a show

BOS- acronym for Best Opposite Sex- judged to be the best rabbit of the opposite sex of the BOB at a rabbit show

BOSV- acronym for Best Opposite Sex of Variety- judged to be the best opposite sex animal of the BOV

BOV- acronym for Best of Variety- judged to be the best broken or best solid at any given rabbit show

Breeder- a term used to describe any rabbit raiser which produces offspring with his or her herd, or a rabbit which is used to breed

Breeding Certificate- a document issued as a proof of a rabbit's ancestry, see also pedigree

BRIS- acronym for Best Reserve in Show- the rabbit at any breed show judged to be the second best overall rabbit

Broken- a white rabbit which is "broken" with fur patches of a different color

Buck- a common name used to refer to a male rabbit

Buck-Teeth- a trait that is usually genetic, which refers to a form of malocclusion in which a rabbit's teeth meet together evenly instead of the upper teeth overlapping the bottom teeth

Bunny Box- a term used to refer to a nest box

Bull Dog- a term which refers to a rabbit with a strong masculine appearance; bold heat, broad shoulders

Cannibalism- the practice of a doe eating her own kits; usually occurs when a doe is overly stressed or when one of her kits dies in the nest box

Carcass- term usually refers to the pelt of a dead rabbit

Carcass Weight- the weight of a rabbit carcass after it has been thoroughly processed

Carriage- the manner in which a rabbit carries or poses itself; generally a showing term

Cheek- the portion of a rabbit's face below its eyes

Chest- the front portion of a rabbit's body between its forelegs and neck

Chopped- a rabbit which lacks overall balance; usually refers to a rabbit lacking in the upper or lower hindquarters

Choppy- see chopped

Class- a group of rabbits that fall into the same gender, pattern and age group

Classification- a system of arranging or identifying rabbits

Cobby- a term which refers to a rabbit with a short and stocky appearance

Cold- a rabbit infection which usually results in repeated sneezing and fluid discharge

Convention- the national or state based rabbit show which is held by ARBA

Crossbred- a rabbit which has direct ancestors from more than one rabbit breed

Crossbreeding- the practice of mating individuals of different rabbit breeds together, producing a crossbred or mixed rabbit; sometimes done with the purpose of increasing a commercial herd's productivity

Crown- the part of a rabbit's head between the ears and behind the brow

Cull- a term given to a rabbit which has undesirable genetic or physical traits; see culling

Culling- the process of eliminating or slaughtering undesirable rabbits from a litter; the term is frequently used by rabbit exhibitors who are in the process of selecting their best show bunnies from a group of litters

D

Dam- a female rabbit which has produced offspring

Dewlap- the flap of extra fat under a rabbit's chin; usually only seen on does

Doe- a common name used to refer to a female rabbit

Domestic Rabbit- a rabbit that has been bred to specifically live in human captivity

DQ- any show rabbit disqualification, trait many times caused by weak genetics

E

Ear Canker- an inflamed scabby condition inside a rabbit's ear caused by an infestation of the ear canal by ear mites; especially common in warm and moist southern climates

Embryo- a kit in the early stages of development inside a doe

Entry- an entry is a rabbit that is scheduled to participate in a particular show

F

Faking- Any technique used to alter a rabbit's appearance before a show

Faults- imperfections which are visible when evaluating a rabbit

Feces- rabbit waste products, manure

Fertility- term refers to a rabbit's ability to "get bred" or simply to reproduce

Finish- the desired degree of perfection in a rabbit's condition; usually referring to fur and flesh condition

Flesh Condition- the condition or firmness of a rabbit's flesh

Foot- the part of the leg on which a rabbit stands

Forehead- the section of a rabbit's head between the eyes and base of the ears

Forequarters- the section of a rabbit's body which begins at the neck and extends to the last rib

Fostering- the process of taking kits from the mother rabbit, and placing them in the nest box of another doe; many breeders have different opinions about this technique

Fryer- a market age rabbit, usually about 10 weeks of age and five pounds in weight

G

Genotype- the genetic makeup of a rabbit, the inherited genes

Gestation- the period of time between breeding and kindling

Grand Champion- a rabbit that has placed first at a rabbit show or at least in its division

Guard Hair- the long and coarse part of a rabbit's coat which offers protection to the undercoat

H

Hormone- any molecule within the body of a rabbit that sends a signal

Hindquarters- the end section of a rabbit consisting of a rabbit's hips, legs, bottom loin and rump

Hip- the thigh joint and large first joint of a rabbit's hind leg

Hock- the middle joint or section of a rabbit's hind leg which is located between the foot and hip

HRS- acronym for the House Rabbit Society, a huge rabbit rescue organization

I

Inbreeding- a breeding program which promotes the mating of closely related rabbits (Example: Brother to Sister, Father to Daughter); surprisingly some studies have shown that limited inbreeding can be very beneficial to your overall rabbit herd... see also Line Breeding

Incisors- a rabbit's sharper front teeth, used specifically for cutting

Inherited- a gene or trait which is passed down from parent to offspring

Inner Ear- the inwardly curved, concave portion of a rabbit's ear

Insemination- the act performed by a buck when he attempts to get a doe pregnant

Intermediate- a rabbit between six and eight months of age in the heavy weight breeds, known as 6-class animals

Inventory- list of all supplies and rabbits that you currently own

J

Junior- a rabbit under six months of age

K

Kindling- the process of giving birth to young offspring

Kit- the proper term for a baby rabbit

Kittens- term refers to multiple "kits" many times of the same litter

Knee- the second joint of the leg which connects the thigh and leg together

L

Lactation- the period of time after kindling when a doe is producing milk

Lapin- the French word for Rabbit

Legs- awards earned by a particular rabbit at an ARBA sanctioned show

Line Breeding- is the purposeful attempt at inbreeding rabbits to a degree, in hopes of producing a better rabbit blood line; when Line Breeding is preformed several from each litter are usually culled

Litter- a mother's offspring, group of bunnies

Live Weight- the weight of a meat rabbit before it is slaughtered for market

Lop- the characteristic of an ear that droops or dangles; generally seen in the lop rabbit

Malocclusion- the misalignment of a rabbit's teeth

Market Age- the age at which meat rabbits are ready to be sent to market; most breeders agree that the best market age for a rabbit is when it reaches 5 pounds

Molting- the process in which a rabbit sheds an existing layer of fur; in warm climates a rabbit usually "molts" during the summer months

Mortality- term referring to death

Muzzle- the projecting portion of the head surrounding the mouth and nose area on a rabbit

Nationals- a national specialty show held by a national specialty club

Nest Box- a box provided to a doe so that she can prepare a nest for her soon to be arriving bunnies inside of it, also called kindling box or simply "bunny box"

O

Open Show- a rabbit show that is open to exhibitors of all ages

Out Breeding- a breeding program which involves the mating of unrelated rabbits of the same breed

Ovulation- the production of eggs by female rabbits; when these eggs are fertilized they can produce embryos

P

Pair- a term that usually refers to a couple of rabbits consisting of a male and a female

Palpation- the process of feeling a doe's abdomen with the hopes of determining whether or not the doe is pregnant

Parasite- an organism that is harmful to the well being of your rabbits

Pathogen- any living organism that causes disease

Peanut- a bunny which has a fatal combination of two dwarf genes

Pedigree- a record keeping paper which shows the ancestry of a given rabbit, normally between 3 and 5 generations are shown

Phenotype- the physical appearance and traits of a rabbit

Processing- the process of slaughtering and dressing a rabbit for market

R

Rabbit Cage- an enclosed structure where rabbits are contained; normally made of wire, sometimes wood

Rabbit Hutch- any enclosed structure in which rabbit are kept; usually made of wood, wire or both

Rabbitry- any place where domestic rabbits are raised or kept

Registrar- a person certified by ARBA to evaluate and "register" rabbits which meet a given criteria

Registration- the process of getting a rabbit registered by an organization such as ARBA

Rex- a medium-sized rabbit with soft fur

Ribs- the curved portions of a rabbit's sides, immediately back of the shoulders and above the belly

S

Sanctioned- shows that abide by ARBA standards and which pay sanction fees to ARBA

Senior- a rabbit over six months of age for 4-class rabbits and over eight months of age for 6-class rabbits

Service- the breeding of a buck with a doe; some breeders occasionally lend each other bucks to "service" each other's does

Shoulders- the uppermost joints of the foreleg which connect it with the body

Sire- a male rabbit which has "fathered" offspring

Smut- term generally refers to the "miss coloration" of fur on a show rabbit

Snuffles- a contagious nasal or lung infection that rabbits can "catch"

Symmetry- an imaginary line down the back of a rabbit which divides the head, ears, legs and body into equal proportions

T

Tattoo- an identification mechanism used to indentify rabbits by the process of placing a letter or number marking in one of their two ears

Trio- generally a "trio" of rabbits consists of three breeding age rabbits; 2 does and a buck

U

Uterus- the name of the organ inside a doe in which developing kits are contained and nourished until birth

V

Variety- a subdivision of any recognized breed class

W

Weaning- a term used to describe the process during which bunnies begin to grow independent of their mother for nourishment; Some breeders will forcibly wean kits between 4 and 8 weeks of age, others leave the bunnies with their mothers for a longer period of time

Wolf Teeth- protruding teeth in a rabbit's upper and lower jaw which is caused by the improper alignment of the upper and lower front teeth, preventing them from being grinded down naturally; generally breeders will automatically cull all rabbits with wolf teeth

Y

Youth Exhibitor- exhibitors under age 19

Made in the USA
Coppell, TX
11 March 2020